THE
MAGICAL MESSAGE
ACCORDING TO
IOANNES
(Τό κατά Ἰωάννην Ἐυαγγέλιον)

THE
MAGICAL MESSAGE
ACCORDING TO
IOANNES
(Τό κατά Ἰωάννην Εὐαγγέλιον)

JAMES M. PRYSE

Athens ‡ Manchester

The Magical Message According to Ioannes

Published by: Old Book Publishing Ltd

Book Cover Design: Old Book Publishing Ltd

Title of original: The Magical Message According to Ioannes

(Τό κατά Ἰωάννην Ἐυαγγέλιον)

Originally published in 1909 by Theosophical Publishing Company
of New York

ISBN–10: 1-78107-167-5
ISBN–13: 978-1-78107-167-0

EDITOR'S NOTE

THE

MAGICAL MESSAGE

ACCORDING TO

IÔANNÊS

(Τὸ κατὰ Ἰωάννην Εὐαγγέλιον)

COMMONLY CALLED

THE GOSPEL ACCORDING TO [ST.] JOHN

A VERBATIM TRANSLATION FROM THE GREEK DONE IN MODERN
ENGLISH WITH INTRODUCTORY ESSAYS AND NOTES

BY

JAMES M. PRYSE

NEW YORK
THE THEOSOPHICAL PUBLISHING COMPANY
OF NEW YORK
244 LENOX AVENUE
1909

TABLE OF CONTENTS.

	PAGE
PREFACE	1
THE SEEN AND THE UNSEEN	7
THE FOUR EVANGELS	31
THE DRAMA OF THE SOUL	41
EXPLANATORY NOTE	59
THE MAGICAL MESSAGE ACCORDING TO IÔANNÊS	71
APPENDIX I., THE PRODIGAL SON	219
APPENDIX II., THE BIRTH FROM ABOVE	223
INDEX OF NOTES	229

PREFACE.

THIS work is a literal translation of the fourth
Evangel, preserving its philosophical and mystical terminology, and, as far as possible, the
peculiarities of its literary form. The modern
English style is followed in this translation, not
only for the sake of clearness, but also because
it fairly represents the simple, homely, and
halting Greek of the *Evangel*. The lack of
English equivalents for many of the Greek
words and phrases makes it impossible to ren-
der these satisfactorily in some passages, but
in all such cases explanatory foot-notes are
added, giving definitions and more adequate
renderings than could be observed in the close
and literal translation. These notes, being in-
dexed, form a glossary of all the important
words in the *Evangel*, thus enabling the reader,
even if unacquainted with the Greek language,
to follow the terminology as closely in the translation as could be done in the Greek text itself,
and affording him almost every advantage to
be had from a study of the original.

The introductory essays and other explanatory matter deal with the philosophical basis and mystical sense of the *Evangel*, without entering needlessly into controversial subjects. That the teaching of Iêsous was largely allegorical is clearly apparent from the subject-matter of the four *Evangels*, as well as from such express statements as that in *Matthew* xiii. 34: "All these things Iêsous spoke to the people in parables, and without a parable he did not speak [anything] to them." That the teaching had an inner and concealed meaning, divulged only to the few who were worthy to receive it, is evident from many passages in the *New Testament;* and it was so held by all the early Christian sects, and plainly admitted by the patristic writers. But, in addition to this allegorical teaching, certain rules of right-conduct are given, which constitute, not a mere arbitrary code of ethics, but one based upon the laws of man's inner nature, his relation to Deity, to Nature, and to his fellow-beings. It is only by living according to these rules of right-conduct that the will of the man comes into harmony with the will of The God; and in *Iôannês* (vii. 17) the final test is laid down: "If any one wills to do *his* will, he shall have knowledge about the teaching, whether it is from The God." Obviously, then, the one thing essential is to lead such a life as will unify the individual consciousness with that which is universal and divine; for there is no other path to spiritual knowledge. True Being can be attained only through right-living, and never through speculation, argumentation, or wrangling over theories. In man, if he will but use them, are spiritual and psychical faculties by means of which he can gain as certain knowledge of the realms of the Soul as he can acquire of the outer world through his physical senses. But the use of these inner faculties is possible only when the whole life of the man is made pure, his heart cleansed from all evil passions, his mind freed from all bigotry and intolerance. The impure heart, the narrow mind, are not fit receptacles for divine wisdom. Mere intellectual assent to an historical record does not make the grave a door to heaven, or constitute Death the unveiler of Life eternal. True knowledge, the direct perception of things spiritual, comes only when right-conduct is followed, and the outer nature of man attuned to the inner and divine nature. The physical body cannot become immortal, nor does the mere disintegration of the body of flesh open the way to immortality. It is the Truth alone that makes man free; and the Truth is not to be known through blind credulity or through contention about beliefs.

It was not till long after the time of Iêsous that the dogmas of Theology were formulated; and so far from these dogmas being based on the teachings contained in the *New Testament*, it is only too apparent that in the translation and interpretation of the *New Testament* every effort has been made to torture it into a confession of such doctrines as eternal damnation, imputed righteousness, and vicarious atonement. This could only be done by maintaining the theory that many of the Greek words in the *New Testament* were used in a new and peculiar sense by its writers. Now, there is no evidence whatever that any such new sense was intended by them; on the contrary, their use of philosophical and other technical terms is very exact, and in strict accord with the meanings found in Greek literature generally. In the present translation, the fictitious theological terminology has been wholly ignored, and each word is translated agreeably with its primary meaning, its natural and obvious relation to the context, and its ordinary signification as used by Greek mystical writers. Accuracy and clearness have been aimed at, rather than mere beauty of language; and the wording of the Greek has been followed as closely as possible in the English, while making full allowance for idiomatic differences.

JAMES M. PRYSE.

NEW YORK, *January*, 1900.

THE SEEN AND THE UNSEEN

THE SEEN AND THE UNSEEN.

CONCERNING Deity and Nature, and the relation of man to both, the teachings of the *New Testament* do not differ from those of any other ancient religious cult or philosophical system. However dissimilar these various systems may be in their external forms of expression, their nomenclatures, symbologies, and formulations, they are yet at one on every fundamental proposition. This essential unity of all the old religions and philosophies is clearly apparent to every one who studies and compares them with a mind open to receive truth from any source and a heart in sympathy with the nobler aspirations of humanity which seek expression in every age. As an introduction to the profoundly mystical and philosophical *Evangel* of Iôannês, a brief summary is here given of the basic concepts common to all the old philosophies, and of the mystical tenets as to the nature of man and his place in the universe, material and divine.

The finite mind can not cognize the infinite Deity, who is beyond all human thought or consciousness, and to be known only through his manifestation in the Universe, of which he is the source and origin. According to Iôannês he is "The God," "the Only One," and the Universe—or "all things," manifoldness springing from the Divine Unity—comes into being through his objectivized Thought, or Logos. Yet even The God is not the unthinkable Absolute, to which ancient philosophy gave neither name nor attributes.

The crude notion that The God is a person who *created* the Universe, which thus had a "beginning," needs but a moment's serious consideration to be rejected. If The God is a person, then he is limited, for that which is unlimited can not be personal. But it is impossible to conceive of ultimate limits to Space, for the instant the attempt is made the mind seeks to fathom what would lie beyond those limits; therefore, if The God were personal, he could not pervade all Space, and there would be regions void of Deity. If The God *created* the Universe, out of what material did he fabricate it? The answer that he created it out of *nothing* is too puerile to be considered; for it means, if it has any meaning, that he did *not* create it out of *anything*, which is equivalent to saying that he did not create it at all. If he created it out of substance already existing, then obviously that substance had existed always, and is eternal; and if it be regarded as "dead" matter, and apart from Deity, then there are two Eternals, and The God is not all-present, for he is not within the "dead" matter, and is but a limited, conditioned Being. The Universe could have had no "beginning" in manifested Time, for Time is but the consciousness of change and transition in the Universe itself.[1]   The "past" is that which no longer exists; the "future" is that which has not yet come into existence; while the "present" is but the dividing-line between these two.   How long is the "present"? The "present day" lies partly in the past, partly in the future; and so of the hour, the minute, the second.   The "present" is therefore infinitesimal, an imaginary dividing-line between the beginningless "past" and the endless "future."

The God is boundless Duration, limitless Space, unconditioned Essence of Being.[2]

The Logos is manifested Time, objectivized Space, differentiated Essence of Being.[3]

[1] The Messenger (*angelos*) . . . swore by him who lives throughout the On-goings of the On-goings, . . . "Time shall be no more." *Rev.* x. 5, 6.

[2] There are many Gods and many Masters; but for us [there is] one Father-God, out of whom [are] all [things], and we [are] in him; and one Master, Anointed Iêsous, through whom [are] all [things], and we through him. I. *Cor.* viii. 5, 6.

[3] All [things] came into being through him, and apart from him not one single [thing] came into being. *Jno.* i. 3.

The Universe is the Illusion of separateness from The God.[1]

The God, unmanifested, is One;[2] in manifestation, threefold.[3] Duration, manifested, is threefold Time; Space, manifested, is three-dimensional; Essence of Being, manifested, emanates three Worlds.[4] Therefore the symbol of Super-Nature, the One and its primary manifestation, is the sacred Four.

Nothing is created: manifestation is a coming out of the Eternal into time,[5] out of the Limitless into embodiment, out of the Changeless into transition. The Within for ever *is;*[6] the Without is for ever *becoming.* The Universe is as boundless as Deity; it is beginningless

---

[1] He was in the world, and through him the world came into being, and the world did not discern him. *Jno.* i. 10.

[2] You believe that The God is One. *Jas.* ii. 19. That Radiance which comes from the Only One. *Jno.* v. 44. God is One. *Gal.* iii. 20.

[3] There are Three who bear witness, the Breath, and the Water, and the Blood; and the Three [are] in the One. I. *Jno.* v. 7, 8.

[4] May your entire [being] — the Breath, and the Psychic-nature, and the [physical] Body — be kept blameless. I. *Thess.* v. 23.

[5] The arcane wisdom which The God pre-appointed *before* the On-goings. I. *Cor.* ii. 7. The On-goings have been adjusted by God's command, in order that the [things] that are seen might be generated from the [things] that do not manifest. *Heb.* xi. 3.

[6] Before Abraham came into being *I am.* *Jno.* viii. 58.

and endless; its matter and force are limitless as to quantity.

Time manifests in cycles, for ever returning upon itself, in days, months, and years, with their fourfold divisions, up to the Four Ages, the future ever becoming the present, yet repeating the past.

In Space the heavenly bodies move along their cyclic paths, measuring time and the seasons.

The Eternal Essence, in the out-going, becomes matter; in the in-going, it re-becomes Divine Substance, in never-ending cycles.

These cycles in Time, Space, and Substance, are the On-goings,[1] or outbreathings and inbreathings of the Divine Life. The First of the On-goings is the Fulness[2] of The God, the totality of all manifestation in Super-Nature. Each of the On-goings is a collective Being, constituted of a host of lesser beings, and the Logos is the synthesis of all these in subjective Nature.[3] In the outermost point of the cycle

---

[1] The God . . . has spoken to us in the last of these days by a Son, . . . through whom also he made the On-goings. *Heb.* i. 1, 2. Not only in this On-going but also in the coming one. *Eph.* i. 21. An unveiling of a Mystery which has been kept in silence in On-going Times. *Rom.* xvi. 25.

[2] It was determined that in him all the Fulness should dwell. *Col.* i. 19. In him dwells all the Fulness of the God-state bodily. *Col.* ii. 9.

[3] He is an image of the invisible God, the firstborn of

of manifestation, these On-goings become the
worlds, suns, planets, races of beings, in periods
of involution and evolution; and the visible
Universe is the sum-total of these in objective
Nature.

Thus there is an endless succession of spheres
of being, worlds outbreathed into Space, and
again inbreathed when their life-cycle is run.
Of these, the ones visible to man constitute but
an infinitesimal part; for the One Substance is
of every degree of tenuity, and but few of its
manifold Elements are perceptible to the physical senses of man, there being states of substance both grosser and more ethereal than
what he recognizes as matter; and these various
states of substance interpenetrate one another,
forming worlds within and without, no point
in Space being void of sentient life.

The Eternal Essence, in its out-going and in-
going, manifests as Spirit; at the point where
the out-going impulse ceases, it manifests as
Matter.   There is no "dead matter" in the
Universe; every molecule of matter must re-

everything embodied; for in him all [things] were embodied, those in the Skies and those on the Earth, those
visible and those invisible, whether Thrones or Master-
ships, whether First-principles or Authorities; all [things]
have been embodied through him and in him; and he is
before all [things], and in him all [things] hold together.
Col. i. 15–17.

become pure spirit. Now, when an On-going—whether a World, the Earth, or a Race — having fulfilled its life-period, is indrawn and disappears from objective Nature, only that portion of it which has been spiritualized returns to the true Essence of Being; that which is imperfect remaining in the spheres of subjective Nature; so that when it is again outbreathed, this residuum, being lowest, is first in manifestation. The new World-period, therefore, opens with Chaos, the Great Deep, the formless elements in Space, holding in latency all that was imperfect in the preceding period. The Light [1] of the Logos, the formative force of the Divine Thought, shining into the Darkness of the turbulent elements, reduces them to order and brings the Kosmos into existence; but this force, energizing all things, awakens the latent imperfect and blind forces of Chaos, which in their synthesis become the Dragon of Darkness, who is the Adversary of the Logos. [2] The Good, the True, the Beautiful, come from the Logos; [3] the evil, the false, the ugly, come from the Chaos.

[1] For everything manifested is Light. *Eph.* v. 13.

[2] The Great Dragon, the primeval Snake, called "Accuser" and "Adversary," who leads astray the whole inhabited world. *Rev.* xii. 9.

[3] The fruit of the Light is in every goodness and truth. *Eph.* v. 9. Every good bequest and every perfect gift is from above, coming down from the Father of the Lights. *Jas.* i. 17.

The God, in his Fulness, is a Divine Unity, unmanifested, yet pervading all things in the three manifested Worlds.[1]

The first of these Worlds, the Spiritual, is that of the Logos, or Divine Ideation, containing the Archetypes of all things that are to exist. It is the model of the Universe as conceived in the Mind of The God.

The second World, the Psychic, is that of conflicting Forces, and is the field of the War in the Heavens, the Hosts of the Logos battling with the awakened Energies of the chaotic darkness. It is the Circle of Inchoation in the Great Deep, the transition-sphere in which all things " come into being" through the formative force of the Logos.

The third World, the Physical, is that of the gross elements, the dregs of Being, the extreme of differentiation or separateness. Though it came into being through the Logos, the divine Light shines into it but dimly, and it is under the sway of the blind, turbulent forces inherent in the gross elements. The Adversary, who is the Leader of the Forces of Darkness, is therefore said, mystically, to be the Ruler of the material world;[2] while the Logos is personified as

[1] One God and Father of all, who [is] over all, and through all, and in all. *Eph.* iv. 6.

[2] The Ruler of the world is coming, and he has nothing in *me. Jno.* xiv. 30.

the Saviour of the world,[1] the only Son of The God offered up as a voluntary sacrifice. Below the elements now manifested are denser states of matter—" *depths* of the Adversary."

Each of these three Worlds reflects the entire process of manifestation, and is therefore septenary in its nature, having realms that correspond to the fourfold inner Deity and to the three stages of externalization. And as three stages on the returning arc correspond to these three out-going ones, there are thus six days of labor, with a seventh of rest. And this sequence holds good of every On-going, whether a planetary system, the Earth, or a Race. Whatever is true of the great cycle is true of every smaller cycle. As The God is The One, so the Universe is The One, or Unity manifesting in Diversity; and the separateness is only in seeming, every part reflecting The One, and a single Law reigning throughout the whole.

The God and all the realms of Nature are mirrored in Man, whose Soul, or True Self, is of fourfold Being, with an appropriate form or vehicle for acting in each of the three Worlds. These four In-beings and three Out-beings are, in the nomenclature of the *New Testament* writers, as follows:

[1] To you is born to-day a Saviour, who is an Anointed Master. *Lk.* ii. 11.

THE FOURFOLD INNER MAN.

1. The God (*ho theos*), the Father.[1]
2. The Primordial Essence, or Origin (*hê archê*), the Mother.
3. The Formative Thought (*ho logos*), the Son.
4. The Breath (*to pneuma*), the Life-principle.[2]

THE THREEFOLD MANIFESTED MAN.

5. The Spiritual Body (*sôma pneumatikon*).
6. The Psychic Body (*sôma psuchikon*).[3]
7. The Physical Body (*sôma*), or "Flesh" (*sarx*).

Incarnated man is thus a septenary being, and a universe in small. In his highest Essence he is one with The God; and in the Divine Realms he is one of the Gods who collectively are the Logos, and who incarnate in the material Universe, or Kosmos, to redeem it. He has share in all the On-goings, and repeats in his own life-periods the whole process of the manifestation of the great Universe, of which

---

[1] "I said, Ye are Gods." *Jno.* x. 34.

[2] If the Breath of him who raised up Iêsous from the dead dwells in you, he who raised up the Anointed from the dead shall make alive also your mortal bodies, through the indwelling of his Breath in you. *Rom.* viii. 11.

[3] There is a psychic body (*sôma psuchikon*), and there is a spiritual body (*sôma pneumatikon*). I. *Cor.* xv. 44.

all the Intelligence, Forces, and Elements are focussed in him. In the highest Realm, the Fulness (*plérôma*), he is the synthesis of all abstract qualities and attributes; as a Masterbuilder in Spatial Life, he is an ideal Form containing all potentialities of forms; in his psychic body are force-centres into which converge all the forces of the World-Soul; even his physical body is an epitome of the material World, its various organs and senses bringing it into relation with every department of Nature. Hence man, in proportion as he comes to a knowledge of himself, becomes a knower of the Universe. Man represents that stage in the progress of Becoming when that which is of a part, the individual, attains to a realization of True Being, the One; and as every part must pass through this stage before the manifested All can become conscious of the Divine Unity, it follows that every being in the Universe is either an incipient, an imperfect, or a perfected Man.

The Soul itself subsists in the One, and abides in the triune Fulness; yet it exists in the three Worlds, energizing man's evolutionary periods in each. Thus incarnated man lives in three distinct domains of manifested Nature. In the Spiritual World he is one of the Planetary Beings, or Solar Gods; in the Psychic World, one of the Lunar Gods, who shape after their

own image the material man, out of the gross
elements of the Chaos or transition-sphere.
Now, the turbulent and evil energies inherent
in these gross elements have to be subdued,
purified, spiritualized; and so the Soul is mystically represented as the Son of The God incarnating in the Kosmos — the physical world,
as also the material body of man — to save it
by taking away its sins.   When the outer man
is purified, he becomes one with his inner and
real Self, and attains to At-one-ment with The
God.   But this purification can not be accomplished in a single Earth-life.   It becomes possible of attainment only after a long cycle of
incarnations, in each of which some portion of
the lower nature may be redeemed.   It is not
the Soul that is to be saved, but the psycho-
physical man.   The Soul is itself the Saviour
and the sacrificial victim; its suffering for the
sins of the elemental self is purely vicarious.

Each incarnation is also a cycle repeating
the whole process of manifestation, detail for
detail, as passed through in the wider cycles of
existence.   On the death of the physical body,
the elements of which return to the sub-human
kingdoms, man passes on into the Psychic
World; yet he can not abide there, as it is only
a transitional stage between the material and
the spiritual.   Here he tarries until he is temporarily purged of the grosser impurities of matter;

and then, leaving in this Lunar Sphere his psychic body as a mere phantom or shade that in time dissolves into the ethereal elements, he goes to the Spiritual World, there resting in bliss ineffable for a period commensurate with the merits of his preceding incarnation. This time of rest ended, he comes again into the transition-sphere, where the same turbulent and impure elements which were for the time discarded are again resumed, a new psychic body concreted, and he is born again into the Physical World, repeating minutely all that takes place in the kosmic and racial cycles.

In the incarnated state, the three phases of consciousness recognized as waking, dreaming, and dreamless sleep correspond to the three Worlds. Even as his consciousness, during the waking state, is centred in the physical body, and through the physical senses is cognizant of material things, so in the dreaming state it is centred in the psychic body, and in the dreamless state in the spiritual body. In sleep man leaves the material form, going to the same realms that he sojourns in after death. In the Psychic World he meets not only the Shades of the recently dead, the ghosts and the phantoms, but also the psychic forms of those who, like himself, are sleeping. There, as in the Physical World, he meets friends, strangers, enemies, among the number of those he knows also on the earth, and others whom he may never meet in the outer life. The same holds true of the next higher World, where he acts in the spiritual body, communing with the Gods and the pure Souls in the resting spheres.[1] And beyond these three states of consciousness is the fourth and highest, that of the True Self.

Now, though man is conscious while acting in the superior Worlds, he is unable, in his present partially developed condition, to carry that consciousness over from one state to the other, and to retain it in his waking memory, owing to the imperfect correlation of the three bodies. The memory of events in the psychic life is impressed upon the psychic brain, but is not transferred to the physical brain, because of the higher rate of vibration of the former. On waking, therefore, he recalls as dreams merely the automatic imaginings of the semi-waking brain, and the confused and distorted reflections from the psychic; yet sometimes impressions are received from the psychic, giving premonition of coming events, and dreams that come true on the outer plane of existence, though usually these impressions are so dim and indistinct that when he comes to places

[1] When at home in the physical body we are away from home from the Master. II. *Cor.* v. 6. I know this very man — whether in the body or out of his body, I do not know. II. *Cor.* xii. 3.

and meets people in the Physical World already known by him in the Psychic, he only has a puzzling sense of familiarity with them, a vague recollection of having come across them before, for which he can not account.

Even more complete is this loss of memory in the wider cycle of reincarnation. The outer man's mind is usually a blank as regards his past lives, and though his relatives and associates are those whom he has known for ages, in many lives in the racial periods of the past, he does not recognize them as such, but looks upon the one short life as complete in itself. The inner man, however, does remember, and tries to revive the friendships, loves, and hates of former earth-lives, to repay past favors and to clear off old scores. Thus man is the slave of his own past, all the incidents of his life, all his relations with his fellow-beings, all the influences brought to bear upon him, being due to causes generated in bygone incarnations; and he is assailed by the evil passions and tendencies of his psychic nature,[1] which is compounded

[1] This knowledge is not [the knowledge] which comes down from above, but [it is] earthy, psychic, mediumistic. *Jas.* iii. 15. We also, when we were children, were enslaved under the elemental-spirits of the world. . . . At that time . . . you were enslaved by those who by nature are not Gods. . . . How is it you are turning back again to the weak and beggarly elemental-spirits ? . . . Are you observing days, and moons, and seasons, and years ?   *Gal.* iv. 3-10.

of the turbulent subtile elements of the transition-sphere, and he is harassed by the brute instincts inherent in the gross elements of his animal body.[1] But beyond all these things which pertain to the spheres of Becoming is the serene God of the man, his Eternal Self in the Realm of True Being, watching over and guiding him, wisely ordering all things for purposes of the purificatory discipline, until at the Perfecting-period the outer becomes as the inner, the below as the above. Then the man has conquered the lower Worlds, and holds the keys of Hadês, the Under-world, and of Death, the Outer-world;[2] in the Over-world he beholds The Father in the mystic Unveiling, the Apokalypsis, and attains to At-one-ment with The God.

Before man can correlate the three Worlds, his whole nature must be made pure. Mere intellectual belief and emotional worship will not effect this. It is a matter of right aspira-

---

[1] I rejoice at the law of The God according to the inner man; but I perceive a different law in my members, making war against the law of my Spirit (*nous*), and taking me captive to the law of sin which is in my members. Wretched man that I am! Who will rescue me from this Death-body? *Rom.* vii. 22–24.

[2] I have conquered the World. *Jno.* xvi. 33. I am the First and the Last, and the Living Self; and I became a dead man, and behold, I am a living one throughout the On-goings of the On-goings, and I have the keys of Death and of the Under-world. *Rev.* i. 17, 18.

tion, right philosophy, right conduct, and of dedication of one's self to The God.[1] Yet if one considers The God as a Being apart from himself, his worship is a negation of the Divine Unity, tending to separate him alike from The God and from his fellow-beings; it is not right aspiration, but glamour arising from the dark and ignorant elements of the Chaos, the Adversary of The God. From this cause come the many religious sects, the divisions, setting man against man, making contention and strife instead of brotherhood and peace. From lack of right philosophy, religious fervor degenerates into blind fanaticism and the prompting to persecute. Right-conduct relates not only to one's duty toward his fellows, but includes mental and physical purity. The functional purification of the physical body results in molecular changes, permitting the psychic forces to act through it, energizing the nervous centres (plexi) and thus correlating the two bodies. This psycho-physiological process is represented mystically by the Lustration of Water, the Water being symbolical of the psychic or magnetic force. The inner senses are awakened, and the man then is capable of conscious action in the Psychic World, retaining memory of it in the physical brain. Following this is the

---

[1] Freed from sin and made subject to The God, you have your fruit in Consecration and Initiation. *Rom.* vi. 22.

Lustration of Fire,[1] the vital electric force, the action of which upon the centres of the brain gives spiritual Seership, the consciousness then being in the spiritual body. Thus the man is "born from above,"[2] becoming "a Son of The God."

But in the evolution of the present human race there was a deviation from the true order, resulting in the degradation of the material form and the perversion of its forces. The first human beings, while yet but lunar entities energizing the subtile elements of the Chaos, were sexless, and moulded forms by the power of Thought and Will alone. But, tempted by the Adversary, the blind instinct of concupiscence inherent in the impure elements, and before the manifestation of the Solar Gods, or spiritual entities, they descended to the gross function of reproduction, which properly pertains only to the lower animal kingdom. Though this function became the normal one, through the natural tendency toward readjustment, its only lawful purpose is the production of bodies in the material World. The original sin was the fall into generation; the unpardonable sin[3]

[1] I indeed lustrate you with Water; but he who is mightier than I is coming; ... *he* will lustrate you in pure Breath and Fire. *Lk*. iii. 16. *Matt*. iii. 11. *Jno*. i. 31–33.

[2] You must be born from above. *Jno*. iii. 7.

[3] All sins shall be forgiven the sons of men, and as many

is the misuse of the generative function. The
result of that fall was the atrophy of the higher
brain-centres; and so intimate is the psycho-
physiological relation between these and the
generative centres, and so delicate the interaction between them, that only the celibate can
pass through the purificatory processes.[1] But
while asceticism and celibacy are possible only
for the few, morality is practicable for all. In
New Testament nomenclature those in the sexual and impure state are termed " the dead ones "
(*hoi nekroi*), because of the atrophy of the spiritual centres of the brain ; and the Resurrection
(*anastasis*) "from among the dead ones " is the
revivification of these atrophied centres which
follows upon the perfect purification of the
psycho-physiological nature.

The human Race, as a whole, constitutes, as
it were, a collective Man ; and its successive
sub-races are analogous to the series of incarnations. At the close of each racial cycle, the

blasphemies as they may blaspheme; but whoever shall
blaspheme against the pure Breath does not have forgive-
ness throughout the On-going, but is liable to separation
for the On-going. *Mk.* iii. 28, 29. *Matt.* xii. 31, 32. *Lk.* xii.
10. I. *Jno.* v. 16.

[1] Unless you turn back and become like little children,
you shall by no means enter the Realm of the Skies. *Matt.*
xviii. 3. There are eunuchs who were born that way from
[their] mother's womb, and there are eunuchs who were

Earth undergoes a geological transformation, making it practically a new globe, and its psychic sphere is likewise renovated. Six great Races succeed each other on the Earth, in six "Days of labor," followed by a seventh and perfected Race in a seventh "Day of rest." Each of these, again, has its sub-divisions; and the men of whom the Race is composed are of different grades, the highest corresponding to the state pertaining to the perfect Race, and these constitute the Initiates, the guardians of humanity's spiritual heritage in knowledge, the Mysteries. As the latter can be imparted only to those men who prove themselves worthy through their efforts toward self-purification, the cycle of instruction in the Mysteries has distinct degrees, the various lustrations in the telestic or perfecting rites. Each racial period, whether great or small, is in itself such a cycle of instruction, and at its beginning a Teacher, one of the number of the Perfect or the Initiates, is sent to preside over it. He is the

made eunuchs by men, and there are eunuchs who made themselves eunuchs for the sake of the Realm of the Skies. *Matt.* xix. 12. The sons of this On-going marry, and are given in marriage; but they who are deemed worthy to attain to that On-going, and to the resurrection from the dead, neither marry nor are given in marriage, for neither can they die any more, for they are like angels, and are sons of The God, being sons of the Resurrection. *Lk.* xx. 34–36. *Matt.* xxii. 30. *Mk.* xii. 25.

"Sun" of that particular Day; and as he represents all the spiritual knowledge which that Race is capable of bringing into manifestation, he is mystically "the Son of the Man." With the beginning of the cycle he founds its Society, entrusts it with the teachings in the various degrees; and when the cycle closes he returns to gather together his chosen ones, or those who, during their incarnations in that Racial period, have held faithfully to the inner spirit of his teachings, and by the saintly purity and unselfishness of their lives have proven themselves worthy to be received into the Assembly of the Perfect.

THE FOUR EVANGELS

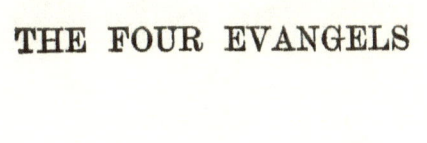

THE FOUR EVANGELS.

THERE is no certainty as to when and by whom the writings now known as the *New Testament* were brought together in their present form and credited to various authors. The arrangement is not very systematic; and undoubtedly some of the works were not written by the individuals to whom they are ascribed, while the real authorship of others is a matter of conjecture. They were selected from a large number of works belonging to the same body of literature, most of which have disappeared. Besides the four *Evangels* contained in the *New Testament*, over fifty others are known to have existed, and some of these were evidently of the greatest value, as shown by the few fragments preserved from the *Evangel according to Philippos* and the *Evangel according to the Egyptians*. Now, Irenæus, in accounting for the selection of only four *Evangels*, states that it was because "there are four Quarters of the World, and four Universal Breaths (*katholika pneumata*)," and because the Cherubim are four-faced. These Cherubim are the "Living

Beings" described in *Ezekiel* (i. 10) as having the face of a Man, the face of a Lion, the face of a Bull, and the face of an Eagle. These four accordingly represented Matthias, Markos, Loukas, and Iôannês, and were formerly depicted at the head of their respective *Evangels*. The reasons assigned by Irenæus may seem fanciful and absurd to those unversed in symbology, yet a profound meaning underlies his words. The four symbols given stand for the four fixed signs of the Zodiac: *Aquarius*, the Water-carrier; *Leo*, the Lion; *Taurus*, the Bull; and *Scorpio*, the "Scorpion monster of darkness," who is said to sting to death, yet to preserve and reproduce, the evening Sun. *Scorpio* is a symbol not only of generation, but also of regeneration and of Seership, the latter being typified by the Eagle, a bird of the Sun. These four are the four "Living Beings" encircling the throne of The God in the *Apokalypse* (iv. 6, 7), in which work the other zodiacal signs, the seven planets, etc., are given, the symbolism being astronomical throughout, and taken largely from the magnificent Mithraic imagery. All external Nature being a manifestation of the inner Deity, the Ancients regarded every natural science as a sacred science, tracing the correspondences between all things in the various' departments of the material Universe and the relations of these to the Divine Realms from which they have their source. The system of the Zodiac is a Mystery-language for expressing the relations and correspondences between the great World (*makrokosmos*), or Divine Man, and the little World (*mikrokosmos*), or incarnated man. A nation being considered also as collectively forming a Man, the territory it occupied was taken to be its body and mapped out accordingly. Thus every ancient country, as Chaldea, Egypt, Peru, Mexico, Druidic Ireland, etc., had its "four quarters," its "sacred city," its "navel of the Earth," etc.; and the body politic, the religious festivals, and the social affairs of the people generally were all instituted on symbolical lines.

The four *Evangels* correspond to the four quarters, and the topography of the Holy Land —"Holy" because devoted to The God through its use as a symbol — is made subservient to the purposes of the allegory. Each *Evangel* is written from a different standpoint, and that of Iôannês is distinct from the three Synoptics. To illustrate the assignment of the four *Evangels* to the three manifested Worlds and the one unmanifested Divine Realm, the symbolizing of these in the embodied Nation, and their correspondences in incarnated man, and at the same time to show the universality of this system in antiquity, a map of the Holy Land is here placed beside one of the carved monoliths found in the prehistoric sacred city near Copan, in Central America.

But three divisions are given in the Holy Land, corresponding to the three outer Worlds; and the fourth, or Divine Realm, is referred to as "beyond the Iordanos." The same distinction is made in the monolith, which has three "heads" representing the three centres in the body, and a fourth above it. Similarly the *Evangel* of Iôannês is considered as being apart from the other three. The correspondences stand as follows:

Iôannês	Eagle	The Plérôma	Beyond the Iordanos	True Self	The "Radiance"
Matthias	Man	Spiritual World	Galilaia	Spiritual Body	Head
Markos	Lion	Psychic World	Samareia	Psychic Body	Heart
Loukas	Bull	Material World	Ioudaia	Physical Body	Navel

In the psycho-physiological rendering of the allegory, the Sea of Tiberias is the ether in the brain; the Iordanos is the vital force in the spinal cord; and the Dead Sea pertains to generation. The three great vital regions in man correspond literally to the three bodies, the physical body coming into being from the lowest centres, the psychic body from the heart-centres, and the sidereal body from the brain-centres. At the one pole is generation; at the other, regeneration, or the mystic birth "from above."

Every event in the four *Evangels* may be

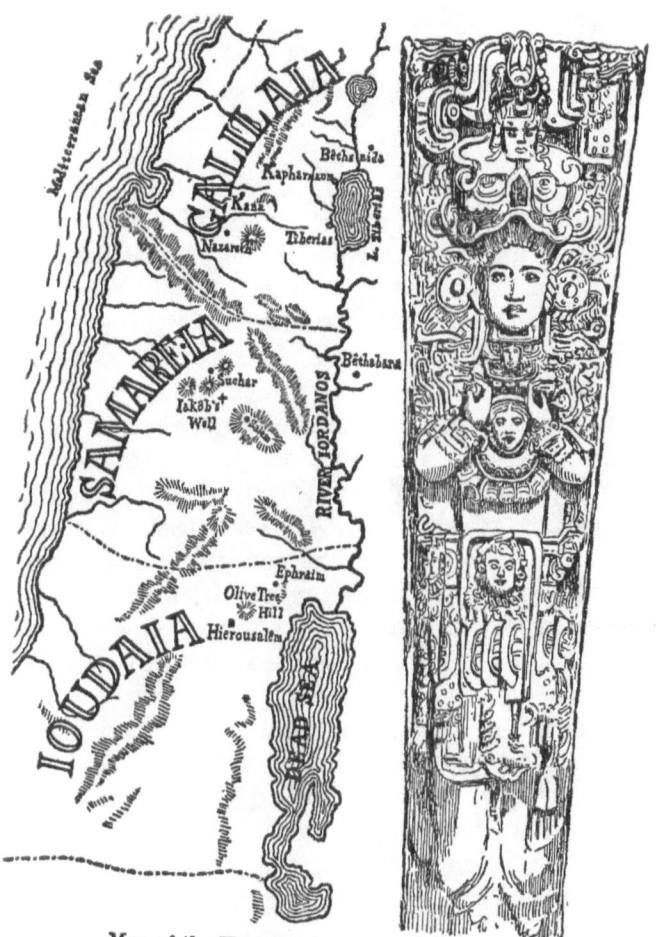

Map of the Holy Land.   Copan Monolith.

read in the language of the zodiacal signs and
the seven planets, yielding an astronomical
meaning; but this is but one out of seven
renderings, from the purely spiritual down to
merely physiological, a series of correspondences running through them all. Nor does
this conflict with the historical basis of the
narrative. None of the events of a man's life
are meaningless, all being the external effects
of interior causes; and in the case of a Divine
Messenger, the Teacher of humanity for a particular cycle, his whole life is an expression of
the inner Realities, a Drama of the Soul. Thus
in the *Evangels* Iêsous is often spoken of as if
he were merely acting a part, doing things "in
order that the Writings might be fulfilled";
yet not because the *Old Testament* Writings
were prophetical in the sense of being mere
predictions of future events in the material
World, but because they affirmed those inner
principles which the Soul is seeking to embody
in the outer life. A mere record of the events
taking place on the material plane of existence
would be of little value as compared with an
allegorical representation of the psychic and
spiritual processes, of the things done in higher
Worlds. The exact date when Iêsous appeared
is unknown. It is not known in what language
he taught. The *New Testament* contains the
only record of his life; and even the fact of his

having lived can not be proved from history. From a mystical standpoint, this is as it should be. The personality of the Messenger is wrapped in obscurity, and the True Self shines forth to the world as an impersonal Light.

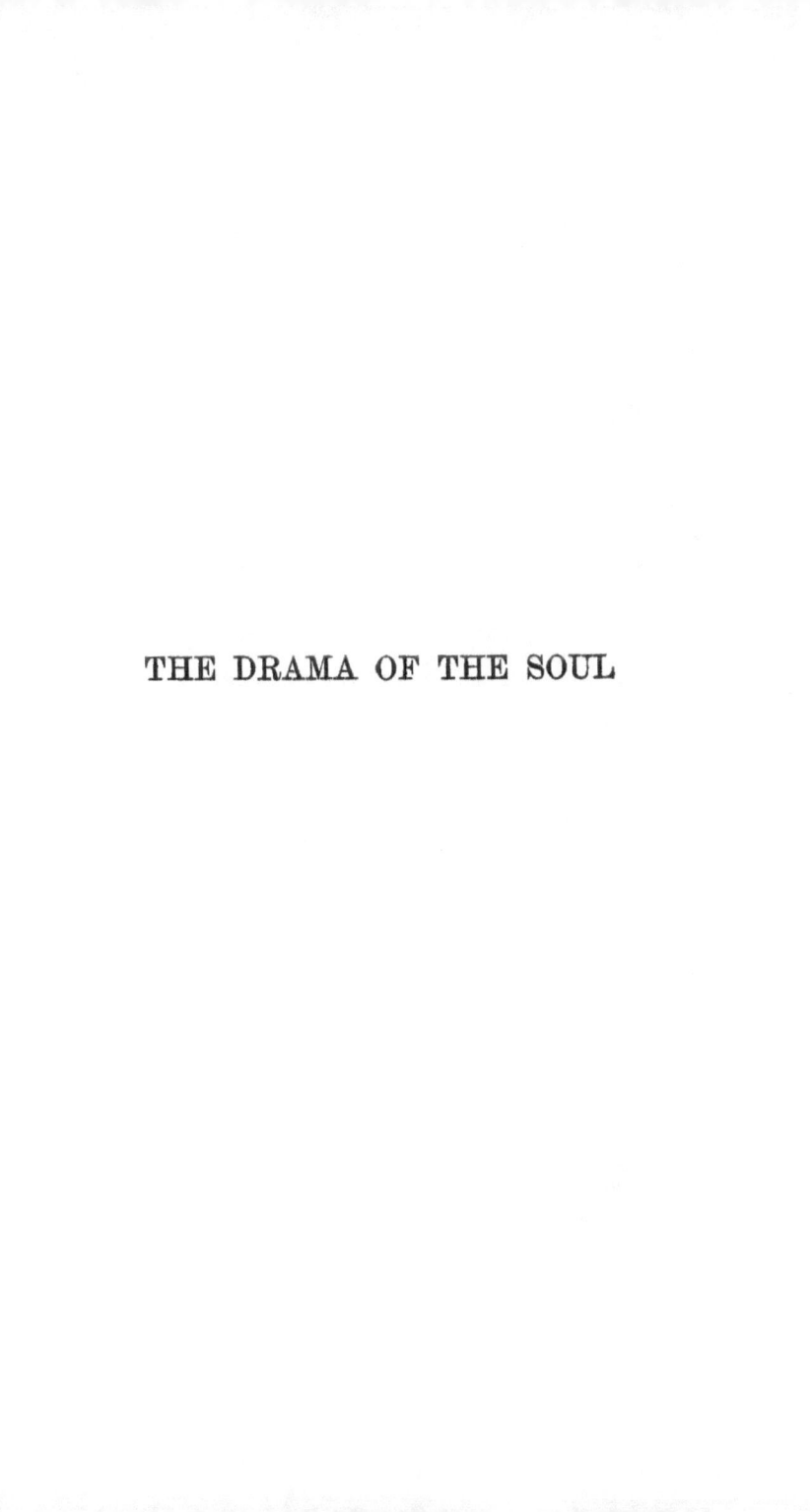

THE DRAMA OF THE SOUL

THE DRAMA OF THE SOUL.

THE *Evangel* of Iôannês opens with a brief recital of the order in which the emanations come into manifestation when a new world-period begins, these emanations being the successive degrees of externalization through which the Universe passes in emerging from its latent state. The manifold Universe, or "all things," comes into existence through the unfolding, or going outward, of the Divine Thought, the Logos. In the Archeus, or universal matrix, is the Logos; in the Logos is the Life; and this Life is the Light of the evolutionary cycles, shining in the Darkness of Chaos. These cycles, or racial periods of objective humanity, are measured astronomically by the divisions of the Zodiac; in the *Evangel* they are termed "Men," for, as each race, like each individual, has its definite life-period, a race may be regarded as a collective being or entity. Further, a Messias or Christos (one "anointed" by the Great Breath or World-soul) appears at the beginning of each such cycle, over which he presides spiritually.[1]

[1] The woman says to him: "I know that the *Messias* is coming, who is called Anointed; when *he* shall have

41

The cycles referred to in the *Evangel* are the twelve divisions or "months" of the sidereal year, or period during which the sun apparently recedes through the twelve signs of the Zodiac, this greater "year" lasting over 25,860 years, and each of its "months" about 2,155 years. The greater year is divided, like the lesser, into four seasons. These lunar cycles are quite plainly indicated in the Biblical allegories: Enoch representing the sun in *Taurus*, Môsês the sun in *Aries*, and Iêsous the sun in *Pisces*. Thus, the dancing of the children of Israel about the golden Calf was simply one of the Mystery-dances, like the *kosmos* dance in the rites of Iacchos, representing the motions of the heavenly bodies; and the destruction of the Calf by Môsês [1] symbolized the passing-over of the sun from *Taurus*, the Bull, into *Aries*, the Ram. During the cycle of Môsês, therefore, the ram and ram's horns became prominent as symbols,[2] and Môsês himself is depicted as having ram's horns on his head, as in one of Michelangelo's paintings. Môsês, in turn, is superseded by Iêsous, whose cycle is that of the sun in *Pisces*, the Fishes, and who accord-

come, he will bring back messages to us." Iêsous says to her: "*I* who am speaking to you am he." *Jno.* iv. 25, 26.

[1] *Ex.* xxxii. 19, 20.

[2] *Ex.* xxix. 1. *Num.* vi. 16, 17. I. *Sam.* ii. 1. *Job* xvi. 15. *Ps.* lxxv. 10; cxxxii. 17; cxlviii. 14.

ingly chooses fishermen for his pupils, performs thaumaturgical feats with fishes,[1] and gives as his Sign that of Iônas, who was swallowed by a great Fish.[2] The original zodiacal sign was the Fish (*piscis*), but because of the occasional intercalary month it was changed to the Fishes (*pisces*). To symbolize the next cycle, Iêsous and the Twelve celebrate the Passing-over in the upper room, the guest-chamber, of the "man bearing a pitcher of water,"[3] who is simply the sign Aquarius, the Water-carrier.

It has been said that the scheme of the Zodiac is due to man's tendency to project an image of himself into space, on the same principle that the heavens, or skies, are regarded as the abode of souls. But this innate tendency arises from the relation of man, the mikrokosm, to the universe, the makrokosm: the soul of man, his higher consciousness, is in reality *universal;* the soul is not subject to time and space, nor

---

[1] *Matt.* iv. 18–22; vii. 10; xii. 39, 40; xiii. 47, 48; xiv. 17–21; xv. 34–37; xvi. 4; xvii. 27. *Mk.* i. 16–20; vi. 38–44; viii. 7–9. *Lk.* v. 4–11; ix. 13–17; xi. 11. *Jno.* vi. 9–14; xxi. 3–14.

[2] A knavish and adulterous generation is clamoring for a sign; but no sign shall be given it except the "Sign" of Iônas the Seer. For as Iônas was three days and three nights in the belly of the great Fish, so shall the Son of the Man be three days and three nights in the Heart of the Earth. *Matt.* xii. 39, 40; xvi. 4. *Lk.* xi. 29, 30.

[3] *Mk.* xiv. 12–15. *Lk.* xxii. 8–13.

does it exist in them, for time and space are concepts of the soul, not objective realities. The perfect man becomes one with the makrokosm, his individual consciousness is merged in the all-consciousness.

The *Evangel* treats, historically and allegorically, of one of these Messianic cycles, and of the Master or Teacher sent to preside over it. This Master (*kurios*) is the Epiphany, or manifestation of the Christos (the Logos or Worldsoul), for the lunar cycle measured by the sun's recession through *Pisces*. Iêsous, the one "anointed" by the Great Breath, is the Saviour during that particular cycle;[1] in other words, the whole spiritual life of the race, all that is possible for it to attain during its racial period, is centred in one individual,[2] who becomes the

[1] This is truly the Saviour of the World — the Anointed. *Jno.* iv. 42. "The Master confirmed by an oath, and will not change his purpose: '*Thou* art a priest throughout the On-going.'" . . . And indeed the greater number [the "silent majority" — the souls of the dead] have become "priests" [intercessors for the living, or "guardian angels"], because of their stay being cut short by death; but *he*, because of his abiding throughout the On-going, has the priestly office that does not pass over [to a successor], and hence he is able to save throughout the whole [world] those drawing near to The God through him, [as he is] at all times and seasons alive to interpose on their behalf. *Heb.* vii. 21-25.

[2] As many of you as were lustrated into the Anointed

exemplar of its spiritual progress, and is therefore in a very real sense "the Path, the Truth,
and the Life."[1] He is the spiritual seed of the
coming race, the prototype of its evolution.[2]
This purely spiritual process has its material
analogy in the physical process of incarnation:
a single germ-cell transmitted by the father
forms the nucleus of a body for the incarnating
Ego, and in its embryonic stages it recapitu-
lates the whole cycle of evolution, assuming
successively the semblance of a stone, a plant,
an animal, and finally the human form, when
it is born into the human kingdom. Yet
man is but a seed-being, as it were, the germ
of a spiritual being.[3] It is for him to be
regenerated, to be re-born into the spiritual
kingdom. He must undergo a transformation as actual as that accompanying physical

were clothed with the Anointed: in [him] there is neither
Jew nor Greek, there is neither slave nor freeman, there is
neither male nor female — for you all are One in Anointed
Iêsous. *Gal.* iii. 27, 28.

[1] I am the Path, and the Truth, and the Life. *Jno.* xiv. 6.
Iêsous, a Forerunner on our behalf. *Heb.* vi. 20.

[2] The promises were spoken to Abraham and to his *seed.*
He does not say, "And to the seeds," as concerning many;
but as concerning one, "And to your *seed*"— who is the
Anointed. *Gal.* iii. 16.

[3] Unless the grain of the wheat falls to the earth and dies,
it abides by itself, alone; but if it dies, it bears much fruit.
Jno. xii. 24.

birth,[1] must be "born from above" into the realm of spirit. The *Messias* is the archetype of this spiritual re-birth.[2]

The *Evangel* of Iôannês, as an allegory, deals with the process of regeneration. And this regeneration is brought about by purifying the whole nature, physical, mental, and moral. It is not the *soul*, but the *body*, that has to be "raised from the dead," to be saved or healed.[3] The body is the instrument through which the soul comes into manifestation in the lower worlds; and the so-called law of evolution is no more or less than the conscious striving of the soul to perfect that instrument. The Divine Self of man, the God, moulds the man of clay, not by the sudden fiat of omnipotence, but by ceaseless toil through many ages; and not until the Perfecting-period is reached and it emerges self-born in the glorified spiritual body, death-

[1] The dead ones shall be raised indestructible, and *we* shall be transformed. I. *Cor.* xv. 52.

[2] The Anointed has been raised up from among the dead ones, a firstling of the sleeping ones. For since Death [came] through a Man, also through a Man [comes] the Awakening of the dead ones. For as in Adam all die, so in the Anointed all are brought to life; but each one in his own band (hierarchy): the Anointed a firstling, afterwards those who [are] the Anointed's in his presence. I. *Cor.* xv. 20-23.

[3] The Greek verb *sôzesthai*, in *New Testament* usage, means equally "to be saved" and "to be healed."

less and free, can it cry, "It is finished," and give up the Creative Breath, as a workman lays down his tools, his task accomplished. The soul itself, as a Divine Idea, is perfect from the first;[1] yet it is but the prototype of that which must come into existence:[2] it must reproduce a perfect image of itself in the worlds of matter, and become one with that image.[3] The physical body, and to a less degree the psychic body, is a congeries of atrophied organs and latent vital centres, functional at one time or another during the vast period of evolution through which the human race has passed, but useless at the present stage; they are, however, capable of being restored to their normal functions, having been preserved or stored up, as it were, to remain dormant until that time, mystically

[1] And *now*, O Father, glorify *me* with thyself, in the glory which I had before this when the world (*kosmos*) *was* with thee. *Jno.* xvii. 5.

[2] Having willed, he gave birth to us by a Logos of Truth, for us to be a kind of firstlings of his embodied beings. *Jas.* i. 18. The first man, Adam, came into being in a psychic form, the last Adam in a life-producing Breath. I. *Cor.* xv. 45.

[3] The Anointed, who is an image of The God. II. *Cor.* iv. 4. As my well-beloved children I admonish [you]; for though you should have countless tutors in the Anointed, yet [you have] not many fathers; for in the Anointed, through the Teaching (*evangelion*), *I* begot you. I. *Cor.* iv. 14, 15.

called the Perfecting-period, when man can take conscious control of the forces of evolution, synthesize all his powers, cleanse and purify his whole nature, quicken and bring into activity all the latent centres of his being, and regain the divine attributes that have been obscured and seemingly lost during the cycles of ages the soul has spent in material existence.[1] Then, and then only, is man "raised from the dead."

That religious truths are thus connected with physiology may appear strange, and even absurd, to a mind trained in modern ways of thinking on religious and scientific questions. If so, it is only because religion has become unscientific, and science irreligious — that is to say, materialistic. Modern science derives psychology from physiology, persevering in the exploded notion that thought is due to the action of the brain; and theology holds to the doctrine of "special creation," asserting that for each body that is born into the world a new soul is created — in other words, that the body precedes the soul. In this, the religious belief is as materialistic as the scientific theory. But in the ancient system the very

---

[1] For you died, and your Life has been hidden with the Anointed in The God. When the Anointed — our Life — shines forth, then *you* also shall shine forth with him in Radiance. *Col.* iii. 3, 4.

reverse is maintained, and physiology is based on psychology: the uncreated, eternally self-existent soul has evolved the physical body as an instrument through which it can manifest itself in the material world; hence, according to this system, function precedes organism in every instance. Every organ represents some quality, power, or faculty of the soul. Whenever any organ has been evolved for a temporary purpose, it becomes atrophied as soon as the energy of the soul is directed into a different channel: it is either laid aside for future use, or is rejected, about as the scaffolding is torn down from a completed structure. The soul is the Logos, or divine Thought, seeking to express itself in terms of matter. But the human brain, in its present imperfect development, can only dimly adumbrate that Thought, the perfect expression of which would make man Godlike in knowledge and power. Hence, in psycho-physiology lies the key to spiritual progress. The gross physical organism, with the animalistic, sensual tendencies retained from a lower cycle of evolution, could not sustain the play of electric and magnetic forces which accompany the noëtic action of the brain, but would be disorganized by the strain. For this reason, great genius verges on insanity. Only when the whole nature of man has become purified from the least taint of his animal propensities can he become the interpreter of the divine Thought, the spokesman of the unseen God.

In the form of a narrative of the events in the life of Iêsous, the incarnate Light, the *Evangel* traces the successive degrees in the purificatory discipline through which the individual Soul must pass to reach the Perfecting-period and attain final emancipation from its prison of flesh. In this purely allegorical rendering, Iôannês and Iêsous are in reality one, being a type of the lunar-solar or psycho-spiritual man; and all the characters in the story are the personified forces of the one man, who conquers all worlds in conquering himself. This was ever the great Drama of the Mysteries, the Sun God crucified, yet rising triumphant from the tomb, self-shining, immortal, conqueror of the Under-world and the World of Death.

The principal events of the narrative, with their psycho-physiological bearing, are given below in the order in which they are found in the *Evangel;* and the subject is further elucidated in the notes accompanying the translation. The astronomical, astrological, and other renderings have been omitted from these notes, which are concerned chiefly with the psycho-physiological meaning of the allegory; for it is only through self-knowledge that real knowledge of external Nature can be gained. It is easy to show that the *New Testament* story, like all the ancient myths, rests on an astronomical basis; but to take this as a final solution of the mysteries of the solar cult is to reach a conclusion that is radically erroneous. For, in turn, the astronomical rendering is itself but an allegory of man's inner life, showing the relations or correspondences existing between the mikrokosm and the makrokosm. These correspondences are actual, not merely fanciful; and the moral meanings conveyed by the myths are only the superficial aspect of the psychic and spiritual realities underlying them.

Iôannês crying aloud in the Desert, "Make straight the Path of the Master," is the psychic self of the man awakening, the precursor of the Spiritual Self that is to come. This forerunner lustrates in water, the magnetic force, which purifies the channels through which the Breath, the electric force, must work when the stage of regeneration is reached. Without the action of this electric force, the living Fire, there can be no real spiritual or noëtic perception; and if this fiery force should be aroused before the channels were sufficiently purified the result would be injury to the brain and nervous system, and even death. It is *vital* electricity; and, while it is the agent of regeneration and a creative force, yet when prematurely awakened and misdirected it becomes destructive, and can kill as instantaneously as a bolt of lightning. In the psychic stages of a man's development the magnetic fluid gradually produces certain changes in the physical body, polarizing the cells and eliminating the grosser elements, and thus prepares the way for noëtic action.

In rapt vision the mystic beholds the "Lamb of God," the Sun-like Self, that spiritual prototype which was himself before his descent into the material world, and which he must re-become when transformed at the Perfecting-period. Having seen that vision, he has placed his feet upon the Path that leads from the human to the Divine.

The Marriage in Kana of Galilaia symbolizes one of the brief flashes of Seership which come to the partly purified mystic long before the complete illumination is attained. The six stone water-jars represent the six lower brain-centres, and the "water" with which they are filled is the magnetic force; the wine, into which the water is converted, typifies the mantic or inspired state of the Seer consequent upon the energizing of the seventh centre, the mystic "third eye." The forces called into action then begin a purifying process in the nervous system, and this is symbolized by the scourge used by Iêsous in clearing the temple-courts.

There is then a change in the magnetic polarity of the body, making it possible to understand what is meant by the "birth from above," and this teaching is put forth in the incident where Nikodêmos comes to Iêsous by night.

At this stage the psychic is able to perceive visually the magnetic colors which emanate from the heart-centres; and this is allegorized in the incident where Iêsous encounters the woman of Samareia at the well which Iakôb gave to his son Iôsêph, who had the *coat of many colors*. Mystically, Samareia is made to correspond to the region of the heart, and Galilaia to the head; and the story of the woman at the well refers to the same process taking place in the heart-region that was represented in the brain by the Marriage in Kana. As only five of these magnetic colors (or rather the forces of which they are manifestations) are as yet developed, the other two being latent and potential, the woman is said to have had five husbands. The separation between the psychic and the procreative centres is noted in the expression "the Ioudaians do not have friendly dealings with the Samareitans," but their close correlation with the noëtic or brain centres is shown by the return of Iêsous to Kana of Galilaia and the healing of the "little

lad" at Kapharnaum—the small but important
plexus in the throat. This separation between
the centres of physical life and the centres of
psychic life is indicated in the Copan monolith,
a plain, unsculptured space having been left
below the psychic region; while a small "head"
represents the synthesizing plexus.

The third stage of purification pertains to the
centres corresponding to the material world;
hence the scene is shifted from Samareia to
Ioudaia. The purifying of these centres is
symbolized by the healing of the sick man at
Hierousalêm, which arouses the enmity of the
Ioudaians, who represent the dark forces of the
elemental self.

The power the ascetic then gains of utilizing
the life-forces of Nature is allegorized in the
story of the loaves and fishes.

The stage of perfect physical purity being
reached, the inner Self forgives the misdeeds
of its outer personality in the past, the latter
being typified by the woman taken in adultery,
who is told to "go, and sin no more."

The illusions of material life having been
overcome, this is mystically represented by
giving sight to the man born blind.

Then follows conscious action in the psychic
body, which is symbolized by Lazaros, who is
raised from the tomb.

The Perfecting-period having been attained,

the noëtic action in the brain is described allegorically in the story of the crucifixion and the subsequent rising-up "from among the dead ones." The glorified Initiate then lives in the spiritual body, exempt from change and death.

The various journeyings and tarryings of Iêsous and the Twelve in the three districts, and the festivals, seasons, days, hours, etc., all have esoteric meanings; and every detail of the allegory is carefully worked out. The discourses and dialogues are in every case explanatory of the incidents in the narrative.

It has been frequently pointed out that the chronology, geography, and the references to Ioudaian customs and religious observances, in the *Evangel*, are not always correct. These apparent inaccuracies are, however, due to the exigencies of the allegory; for the "days" and "hours" of Iôannês refer to psycho-physiological cycles, and he introduces the Ioudaian festivals and customs into his narrative only in their esoteric meaning. Even if he does place a town "on the other side of the Iordanos" when in fact it was on the hither side, the mystical meaning loses nothing by the geographical error.

EXPLANATORY NOTE

EXPLANATORY NOTE.

THE word *evangelion*, which is used as part of the title to each of the first four books of the *New Testament*, means primarily the reward given to a messenger who brings good tidings, and secondarily the message that he brings. But the ordinary Greek word *angelos* ("messenger") was converted by the *New Testament* writers into a technical term to replace the word *daimôn*, the latter word having become degraded. The Angels of the *New Testament* are the *daimones* of the older Greek religion. The word *daimôn* meant the Divine Essence, the Oversoul or Ruling Power of the Universe; and the *daimones* were the conscious creative and energizing Powers, of every degree, from the demigods or tutelary deities down to the nature-spirits or *genii;* and all these, whatever theology may say to the contrary, are *souls* in various stages of development, whether the souls of the mighty dead of past ages, "the spirits of just men made perfect," or "ministering Angels," the overshadowing souls of men

still in the flesh, or the lower orders of spiritual
beings that have not yet "been born in human
shape." As the word had come to mean merely
the shades or ghosts of the dead, it is so used
in the *New Testament*, where it is almost invariably applied to *larvæ*, the unclean spirits or
psychic phantoms of the dead, which obsess
impure and mediumistic persons. The primary
meaning of *daimôn* having been transferred to
the word *angelos*, the derivative *evangelion* acquired likewise a new meaning: it is a Message
from, or concerning, the World of Souls, the
realm of the Logos, or Divine Ideation; in
other words, it is a Magical Message or teaching. The four *Evangels* are, in fact, treatises
on practical Magic, not, however, Thaumaturgy,
or Wonder-working, but Theurgy, the Divine
Work of self-purification, to be accomplished
through the mystic Lustrations in the telestic
or perfecting rites. The exaltation of the thaumaturgic element by the ecclesiastics (who had
lost the "key of the Gnôsis," if they ever pos-
sessed it), with the later theological development of the belief that "miracles" were hap-
penings outside of and beyond the realm of
Law, followed naturally upon the formulation
of a dualistic theology which places Deity apart
from Nature and from man, and which, under
the guise of Monotheism, advocates in reality a
most unphilosophical Polytheism, making Good

and Evil absolute principles, and deifying both.
According to this polytheistic system, a good
God and his Angels, or lesser Gods, reign eternally over the abodes of bliss, while a bad God,
the Devil, and his Demons, or evil Deities, preside over the regions of everlasting woe. This
error of considering The God to be separate
from Nature, instead of his being, as Paulos
asserts, consistently with the belief of all antiquity, "the *one* God energizing all things in
all," has led to the perversion of religion, the
limitation of science, and the obscuration of
philosophy. The baseless assumption that the
Christian Mysteries differed from the so-called
Pagan Mysteries — whereas, on the contrary,
the real Mysteries are ever the same — resulted
in the deliberate concealment of the fact that
the *New Testament* writings abound in mystical
terms and imagery taken from the Pagan Greek,
Mithraic, and other arcana; yet without a
knowledge of the esoteric meanings of these
terms and images the writings themselves are
almost wholly incomprehensible.

In the translation of *Iôannês* here presented,
all the principal words that have an arcane
sense are carefully defined in the foot-notes;
words which are emphatic in the Greek are
italicized in their English rendering, a matter
of importance in this *Evangel*, in which the
meaning often depends upon peculiarly em-

phatic phrasing; and words necessary to complete the sense in the English idiom are bracketed. Place-names and names of persons are given in their Greek form, to avoid the inconsistencies of the authorized version, which gives them in forms Anglicized from the Latin, with sporadic attempts to refer them to the Hebrew. The text is taken mainly from the oldest manuscripts, the principal variations in their readings being given in the foot-notes.

Although there are about a thousand Greek manuscripts of the *New Testament* extant, only thirty of them contain the whole of it, and only five — including the Greco-Latin Beza, which

HCENCHMEIONΧ
ΓΟΝΟΥΤΟСΕСΤΙΝ
ΑΛΗΘωСΟΠΡΟΦΗ
ΤΗСΟΕΙСΤΟΝΚ·ω
ΕΡΧΟΜΕΝΟС·
ΙС·ΟΥΝΓΝΟΥСΟΤΙ
ΜΕΛΛΟΥСΙΝΕΡΧ
СΘΑΙΚΑΙΑΡΠΑΖΕΙΝ
ΑΥΤΟΝΚΑΙΑΝΑΞ
ΝΑ ΚΗΝΥΝΑΙΒΑСΙΛΕΑ
Δ ΦΕΥΓΕΙΠΑΛΙΝΕΙΤ
ΟΡΟСΜΟΝΟСΑΥΓ

Codex Sinaiticus. *John* vi. 14, 15.

has only the four *Evangels* and the *Acts* — can with certainty be assigned to a date earlier than the tenth century; and while these five are supposed to belong to the fourth and fifth centuries, they may have been made at a much later date. These manuscripts are:

The Sinaitic, now at St. Petersburg. It was discovered, in 1844 and 1859, by Professor Tischendorf, at St. Catherine's Convent (at the

Codex Alexandrinus. *John* i. 1–7.

foot of Mount Sinai), part of it being in a basket of litter given him to light his fire. It contains, in addition to the commonly received writings, the *Epistle of Barnabas* and the *Shepherd of Hermas*, and is an exceedingly careless and inaccurate copy, made by a scribe whose knowledge of Greek was evidently very limited. It contains corrections in a different handwriting, probably added in the sixth century.

The Alexandreian, now in the British Museum. It is incomplete, and shows many traces of the knife and sponge used in making changes and corrections. It omits *John* vi. 50–viii. 52.

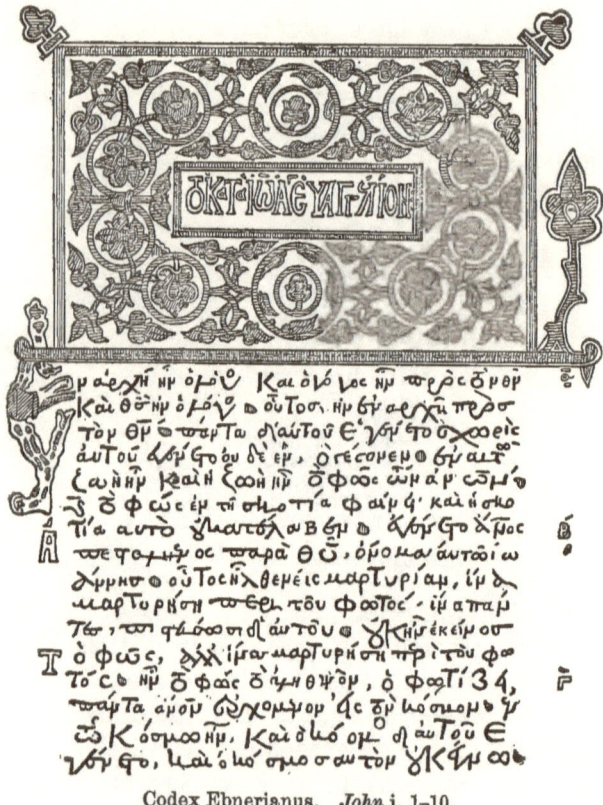

Codex Ebnerianus. *John* i. 1–10.

The Vatican, No. 1209 in the Vatican Library
at Rome. It is very corrupt, has evidently
been tampered with, and is remarkable for
omissions, lacking the *Apocalypse, Hebrews* ix.
4 to the end, I. and II. *Timothy, Titus,* and

Philemon. It divides *John* into eighty chapters, and omits vii. 53–viii. 11.

The Ephrem, now in Paris. It is a palimpsest, and very incomplete, wanting nearly half of the *Evangels* and about a third of the rest of the *New Testament.* It divides *John* into eighteen chapters.

The Beza, now in the University Library at Cambridge. It is a Greek and Latin copy of the four *Evangels* and the *Acts,* and is very corrupt, containing extensive interpolations — more of them, in fact, than any other known manuscript.

Of these five manuscripts, the Beza is supposed to have been made in Lyons, France, and the four others in Alexandreia, Egypt. All the older manuscripts are written entirely in capitals (uncials), with no divisions between the words except at new paragraphs, and with few, if any, marks of punctuation. The later manuscripts are mostly cursives, that is, written in running hand. The present division into chapters and verses was made probably not earlier than the thirteenth century.

The English authorized version (King James's Bible), first published in 1611, is little more than a revision of, and by no means an improvement upon, the translation made from the Latin *Vulgate* by William Tyndale, and published in 1526. For, while that version was based, by

order of the king, upon the "Bishops' Bible,"
and the "former translations" were "diligently
compared," all these translations, with the ex-
ception of the Roman Catholic version (which
was confessedly Englished from the *Vulgate*),
had been cribbed from Tyndale's admirable
work. And while Tyndale's version is commonly said to have been from the original, he
himself never made that claim. That it was
done from the *Vulgate* is shown conclusively by
numerous errors in translating, of a sort that
would easily be made from the Latin, but that
would be unaccountable if the translator were
following the Greek text. The credit for the
literary beauty of the English version is due
almost wholly to Tyndale. But over twenty
thousand errors have been pointed out in the
King James Bible; and the revised version,
while correcting many of the more glaring of
these inaccuracies, has perpetrated others
equally bad, besides destroying the rhythm in
many passages, and changing the diction to an
incongruous mixture of Elizabethan and modern
English. In this respect, however, it resembles
the text of the original, especially that of the
Apokalypse, which represents the Greek of two
distinct periods, separated by centuries. On
the whole, the English *New Testament* is inferior
to the Spanish version of Cipriano de Valera,
first published in 1602. Accurate and merito-

rious translating, like original composition, is necessarily the work of the individual, who can become absorbed in his subject and not be interrupted or hindered while seeking to give it adequate expression. Any translation made by a committee, even by an "assembly of divines," is sure to be a colorless rendering, produced from lexicons by a process of mere word-change, and consequently but a poor and lifeless literary performance.

THE MAGICAL MESSAGE ACCORD-
ING TO IÔANNÊS

THE MAGICAL MESSAGE ACCORD-
ING TO IÔANNÊS.

In a First-principle[1] was the [uttered]
Thought,[2] and the Thought was in relation to

[1] Gr. *archê*, first cause, inherent principle of evolution as
opposed to the primary elements (*stoicheia*), which are the
first differentiations of the root-substance. It is the divine
spirit of Life pulsating through Chaos, or Space. Considered
as the kosmic matrix, or womb of the world, it was symbolized by the crescent moon (typical of female generative
power), and by the ark, or ship of life, floating on the " Great
Deep," or watery abyss of Space, and preserving the germs
of all living things during the intervals between the periods
of kosmic objectivity. Colloquially, *en archê* means " at
first," or " in the beginning "; but here the word has the
same philosophical meaning it has in *Heb.* vi. 1 : " Leaving
the discussion (*logos*) of the First-principle (*archê*) of the
Christos, let us refer to perfection [initiation]."

[2] Gr. *logos*, the external expression of the interior thought,
and the thought itself; a saying, oracle, divine revelation ;
a " word " as the embodiment of an idea, but never in the
grammatical sense as the mere *name* of a thing. The Vulgate mistranslates it *Verbum*, " Word "; but the Beza has
Sermo, " Speech "; and Tertullian (*Apol.* c. xxi.) gives *Sermo
atque Ratio*, " Speech and Reason." The Logos is the Divine

The God,[1] and the Thought was a God.[2] This [God] it was who in a First-principle was in relation to The God. All [things][3] came into

Thought, which, impressed upon the primal substance (*archê*), is alike the pattern and the formative force of the universe. It is, therefore, the Archetypal World, containing the Ideas or Souls of all things. The Logos and the Absolute Principle (*archê*) are the two aspects of the One.

[1] Gr. *ho theos*, probably from the older form *Zeus* — the Father of the Gods and of men; but still not Absolute Deity, the Unmanifested, the incognizable "Only One." " The God " is a collective term for all in the purely spiritual worlds.

[2] Gr. *theos*, without the definite article, in contrast with *ho theos*, The God. The distinction is clearly indicated also in the preceding phrase (which is emphatically repeated), "in relation to The God," *pros ton theon*, where the preposition *pros* — though commonly translated "with," out of deference to theological notions and in defiance of Greek — has somewhat of an adversative force; in fact, it would be good Greek for "in spite of The God," while the rendering " with God " is untenable. In *Rom.* xv. 17 and *Heb.* ii. 17 the phrase is used, *ta pros ton theon*, " the [things] relating to The God." The conception in the text is unmistakably identical with that of Philo Judæus, who speaks of the Logos as "the Second God" (*De Somn.* i. 655) and makes him the synthesis of all the spiritual powers acting upon the kosmos. Hermês Trismegistos also (quoted approvingly by Lactantius, *Divin. Instit.* iv. 6) calls the Logos " the Second God "; he moreover makes the same distinction between *theos* and *ho theos*, calling the Logos " a God " to distinguish him from The God. Justin Martyr held the same view, using the term "Second God" (*deuteros theos*), and so did Origen.

[3] Gr. *panta*, all ; here used absolutely, the whole kosmos.

being[1] through him, and apart from him not one single [thing] came into being. That which has come into being was Life[2] in him, and the Life was the Light of the Men[3]; and

---

[1] Gr. *ginesthai*, to become, to come into objective existence, to come out of the Eternal into Time, as contrasted with *einai*, to *be;* to be born. The God is boundless Duration, which neither *is* nor *is not;* the Logos is Time in the abstract, which eternally *is;* the kosmos, in manifested Time, is ever *becoming.* Nothing is " created " or " made," but all things emanate from the Eternal Essence (*ousia*), and pass through the Sphere of Transition (*genesis*) into the Differentiated World (*kosmos*). See Appendix I., " The Prodigal Son."

[2] Gr. *zóé*, life, as opposed to death. Life is also the Breath (*pneuma*). In kosmic manifestation it is the Solar Energy, which visually is Light. The punctuation of the text as above is incontestably the correct one, having the support of a majority of the orthodox church fathers as well as of all the so-called " heretics." The punctuation which severs the words " that which became " (*ho gegonen*) from the sentence to which they belong, and joins them in a meaningless way to the preceding sentence, is a futile attempt to conceal the fact that Life (the Breath) is one of the Emanations that come into being *in* the Logos. All the ancient authorities prove that the stop should be placed before *ho gegonen*, and the whole sense of the passage clearly shows this to be the true punctuation.

[3] The Men are the twelve zodiacal signs — in the astronomical rendering — the twelve " Patriarchs " of the *Old Testament;* the twelve months of the year, whether a year of mortals, or the sidereal year of about 25,000 years, or a year of the Gods, the whole lifetime of the kosmos. The zodiacal signs are alternately diurnal and nocturnal, making six periods of activity as day and night.

the Light illuminates in the Darkness,[1] and the Darkness did not overtake it.

There came into being a Man sent forth from [the Light-giving] God; his name [was] Iôannês. This [forerunner] came for witness,[2] that he might bear witness about the Light, that all might have faith [3] through him. *He* was not

[1] The principle of duality, good and evil. Darkness is the chaotic element, that blind, turbulent energy in matter which is the source of all " evil." The imagery in this passage is solar, referring to the ancient mythos of the dragon of darkness pursuing the sun to devour it, but never able to overtake it. The verb used, *katalambanein*, means to catch, to come upon, to overtake; in the middle voice it is used in the *Epistles* in the sense of comprehending mentally, but in the active voice, as here, it can not have that meaning. The word is used also in the passage, " Walk while you have the Light, so that Darkness may not overtake you " (xii. 35).

[2] One who can retain in his physical consciousness the memory of things in the psychic and spiritual worlds is said to " bear witness " when he declares them to men who can not so remember, to help revive their dormant psychic faculties.

[3] Gr. *pisteuein*, to trust in, to rely on, to have conviction; from *pistis*, assurance, good-faith, credit (in business affairs), a pledge, an argument, a proof; the power of the soul to appropriate knowledge; the intense fervor springing from a conviction of the reality of the spiritual life; in a philosophic sense, certain knowledge based upon *intuitive perception* gained by correlating the physical body with the psychic. Those who had the faculty of *pistis* were called the psychics (*psuchikoi*), as distinguished from the spiritually regenerated men (*pneumatikoi*) on the one hand, and

the Light, but [he was sent] that he might bear
witness about the Light. [The Thought] was
that True[1] Light which, when it comes into the
world,[2] lights every Man.[3]   He was in the world,

the carnal or earthy men (*sarkikoi, choïkoi*) on the other.
While *pistis* is psychic knowledge rather than spiritual, it
is by no means blind faith or unreasoning opinion. For
lack of an English verb to convey its exact force, *pisteuein*
is here translated, in a few passages, "to have faith."
The word *pistis*, however, does not occur in *Iôannês ;* and,
curiously, *pisteuein* is not used in the *Apokalypse*.

[1] Gr. *aléthinos*, the *real*, as opposed to the *apparent*. At
the beginning of each of the Life-Cycles there is an out-
shining of the Light, and a *Messias* (one anointed by the
Breath) appears as the spiritual Teacher of mankind for
that particular cycle. The cycle of Iôannês-Iêsous (for
the two are really one, the psycho-spiritual man) was that
of the Sun in the sign Pisces, the Fishes. Mikrokosmi-
cally, Iôannês is the psychic or magnetic light which precedes, and prepares the way for, the True Light, the noëtic
or spiritual illumination.

[2] Gr. *kosmos*. The primary meaning of the word is
" good order," and it is applied to anything having definite
form or arrangement, from an ornament, or a fashion in
dress, to the whole manifested universe. Chaos, or rather
the primary matter it contains *(hulê*, unwrought material),
becomes, through the formative power of the Logos, the
kosmos or objective universe, each department of which is
also a kosmos or world in itself; hence the word applies
to the suns and planets in space, to this earth, to humanity
in general, and to individual man.

[3] The construction of this sentence, in the Greek, is very
confused, and leaves it uncertain whether "coming" refers
to the "Light" or to "every Man." Hence it may also be

and through him the world came into being,
and [yet] the world did not know him. He
came into the [things] that were his own, and
they who were his own[1] did not take[2] him [to
themselves]. But as many as did receive[3] him,
to them he gave authority to become children
of [the manifested] God (to those having faith
in his Name[4]), who were born,[5] not of human
parents[6] (neither of the will[7] of [a woman's]

construed either, "That was the True Light which lights
every Man coming [or, "when he comes"] into the
world"; or, "That True Light, which lights every Man,
was coming into the world." If the latter is intended, the
allusion would be to the manifestation (*epiphaneia*) of the
Logos at the beginning of each cycle, the advent of a Messias.

[1] Gr. *ta idia*, one's own possessions, one's home; and *hoi
idioi*, one's own relatives, friends, or people.

[2] Gr. *paralambanein*, to take from (the sender); to take
to one's self. Man came into existence through the Logos,
but remains in ignorance of his own true nature, does not
become one with his inner God.

[3] Gr. *lambanein*, to take hold of, make one's own; to en-
tertain, receive hospitably.

[4] The "name" is the *Amên*, which has no meaning as a
word, its whole potency being in the *sound*. See note 3, p. 88.

[5] Literally, "begotten"; but in later Greek, as here, the
verb used means rather "to be born."

[6] The Sinaitic and the Beza read, "blood-relations" (literally, "bloods"). The authorized version gives "blood,"
which is misleading.

[7] That is, *will* as *desire*, the creative impulse; thus *Jas.* i.
18: "Having *willed*, he gave birth to us by a Logos of
Truth."

flesh nor of the will of a man[1]), but of [the man-ifested] God. And the Thought became flesh, and encamped among us; and we beheld his Radiance,[2] a Radiance as of a [son] born of one [parent] only[3] (from a father), full of Grace[4]

[1] Gr. *anêr*, man (as distinguished from woman). The parenthetical clause merely emphasizes the preceding state-ment that the Logos-born are not of human parentage.

[2] Gr. *doxa*, opinion, *subjective* knowledge (as opposed to objective); self-opinion; honor, glory; a fancy, dream, vision; generally used by the *New Testament* writers in the sense of *splendor*, brilliant shining, to denote the lumi-nous cloud or *aura* enveloping the purified man or Initiate, and which is visible only to the inner sight. It is the " flesh " of the Logos, the substance of the spiritual body or Augoeidês (the " Light-like " form). The expression " encamped among us " (literally, " pitched tent ") refers to this luminous envelope.

[3] Gr. *monogenês*, born of one only; hence the explana-tory phrase, " from a father." (A variant reading has, " a God born," etc.) The spiritually regenerated man is self-born, that is, born from himself as his own father, in the deathless spiritual body. The term was applied to Zeus and other Sun-Gods; for the sun is a type of perfect man, and the earth a type of unregenerate man, the planets being regarded as embryonic suns, and the sun as a per-fected planet. The word is consistent with the solar imagery used in this *Evangel*, and is not applied in the Synoptics to the Christos. *Monogenês* also means " beget-ting but one " and " only begotten " or " only." In the latter sense it is used in *Luke* vii. 12, " an only son of his mother, and she was a widow."

[4] Gr. *charis*, that which gives joy: (subjectively) kind-ness, gratitude; (objectively) beauty, loveliness.

and Truth.[1]　(Iôannês bears witness about him, and cried aloud, saying, "This [Light] it was of whom I said, He who is coming behind me has come to be in front of me, for he was my First."[2])　For from his Fulness *we* all received, and Grace for Grace.　For the Law[3] was given

[1] Gr. *alétheia*, the Real (as opposed to the apparent, the false); the changeless spiritual basis upon which come and go the illusionary forms of the transitory world.

[2] Or, "prototype." The lunar Gods evolve the physical forms of men, in which the solar Gods incarnate later on; yet the latter are the prototypes preëxisting in the archetypal world.　Here, Iôannês represents the lunar man (*psuché*), and Iêsous the solar man, or spiritual Self.　The sentence here placed in parentheses interferes somewhat with the meaning, and is inserted in some manuscripts after verse 18 (at the end of the paragraph above).　The Radiance is the root-substance of the archetypal world; it is "full of Grace and Truth," and this Fulness (*plérôma*) is the totality of all the abstract qualities of the World-soul.　The words "Grace for Grace" express the interaction between the higher and the lower worlds, and the relation of the mikrokosm to the makrokosm.　As ideal Space, of three degrees corresponding to the three dimensions in manifested Space, the Plêrôma is the "house of the Father," and the abode of divine beings and pure souls.

[3] Gr. *nomos*, that which is assigned, or apportioned; custom, conventionalism; law, ordinance.　The Mosaic Law consists of ritualistic observances based upon the action of the forces ruling the material world.　It is the law of cause and effect inherent in the elements (or, rather, the *spirits* of the elements) that keeps the soul in bondage in the world of matter, and holds it within the cycle of reincarnations, the mind being attached to the objects of the

through Môsês; the Grace and the Truth came into being through Anointed [1] Iêsous. No one has ever yet seen *God*[2]; the Self-born[3] Son, who is in the bosom of the Father, *he* it is that explained[4] [him].

senses and to the results of actions. From this bondage the soul can become free only by purification and the acceptance of the "free gift" of the Logos, when it is re-born in the divine Essence and becomes "the Son of a God." Thus Paulos says (*Gal.* iv. 3–8) : "We also, when we were youngsters, were enslaved under the elemental-spirits (*stoicheia*) of the Kosmos. But when the Fulness of the Time came The God sent forth his Son, born from a woman, born under Law, that he might ransom those under Law, so that we might regain the Sonship. And because you are Sons he sent forth the Breath of his Son into our *hearts*, loudly calling, '*Abba*, Father!' So that y o u are no longer a Slave, but a Son, and if a Son, also an heir of a God; but at that time, indeed, not perceiving a God, you were enslaved by those who by origin are not Gods."

[1] Gr. *christos*, washed, anointed with oil (after bathing). Mystically, one is said to be "anointed" when he has been purified by the Breath. In the Mysteries there was an actual anointing with oil (usually palm-oil) to which magical virtues had been imparted; and preparatory to the purification by Fire an oil extracted from asbestos was used.

[2] That is, the Logos, or "second God," as the Unmanifested Thought (*logos endiathetos*).

[3] Gr. *monogenês*. See note 3, p. 77.

[4] Gr. *exêgeisthai*, to expound, to teach, to act as interpreter for a God; especially, to interpret omens, oracles, and ritualistic ceremonies.

And this is the witness of Iôannês, when the Ioudaians sent to him from Hierousalêm[1] priests and Levites to ask him:

" Who are *y o u*[2]?"

And he admitted, and did not deny, and admitted:

"*I* am not the Anointed."

And they asked him:

" What, then, [are y o u]? Are y o u Hêlias[3]?"

---

[1] Also spelled "Hierosoluma." Originally, an Euphratean place-name meaning " City of the God of Peace." Oannês (*Ea-khan*, " Man-Fish ") was called *Sallimmanu*, "the God of Peace," whence the Biblical " Solomôn" (*Sheloumouh*).

[2] To distinguish the singular pronoun from the plural, it is spaced thus, y o u.

[3] There is a play here upon the words Hêlias and *hêlios*. Iôannês evades the question, " Are y o u Elijah (*Hêlias*)?" by taking it to be, " Are y o u the Sun (*hêlios*)?" and therefore answers, " I am not." In *Matt.* xvii. 11-13 it is positively stated that he was the reincarnation of Hêlias (Elijah): " Now, Iêsous answered and said to them: ' Hêlias indeed comes first, and shall restore all [things]. Now, I say to you, Hêlias has come already.' . . . Then the pupils understood that he said [this] to them about Iôannês the Lustrator." Hêlias is described in II. *Kings* i. 8 as " a hairy man, and girded about the loins with a girdle of skin "; and he is said to have killed two bands of soldiers by calling down fire from the sky — a bit of black magic. Reincarnated as Iôannês, he is thus described in *Matt.* iii. 4: " Iôannês wore a garment of camel's hair, and a girdle of skin about his loins "; and for the evil deed of that former incarnation Nemesis pursues him, in the person of the wanton Hêrôdias, and he is beheaded. Most of the char-

And he said:

"I am not."

"Are you the Seer[1]?"

And he answered:

"No."

Therefore they said to him:

"Who are you?—that we may give a reply to those who sent us. What do you say about yourself?"

Said he:

"*I* [am] 'The Voice of one shouting in the desert, "Make straight the path of the Master,"' as said Hêsaias the Seer."[2]

---

acters in the *New Testament* story may be traced through a number of incarnations in the stories in the *Old Testament*.

[1] Gr. *prophêtês*, one who speaks for (another), especially for a God; the interpreter of a God, a seer. Here the Seer Hêsaias (Isaiah) may be intended, as suggested by the context following; but more probably Hieremias (Jeremiah) is meant, since he is named in *Matt.* xvi. 14 as one of the seers whom the people were expecting to reincarnate among them at that time. But in the parallel passages in the other *Synoptics* (*Mark* viii. 28; *Luke* ix. 19) Hieremias is not mentioned. The expectation of the coming of Hêlias was based upon *Mal.* iv. 5: "Behold, *I* send you Hêlias, the divinely frenzied one, before the great and manifested day of the Master comes." And as in this prophecy the *Messias* is called "the Sun of Righteousness," the play on the words *hêlios* and *Hêlias* is natural enough.

[2] *Isa.* xl. 3. The subjective consciousness, realized only through interior contemplation, is the "path" which extends between man's personal self and his inner God.

And they who were sent were from among the Pharisaians [1]; and they questioned him, and said to him:

"Then why do y o u lustrate,[2] if y o u are not the Anointed, neither Hêlias nor a Seer ?"

Iôannês answered them and said:

"*I* lustrate in Water [3]; but in your midst

[1] The principal sect of the Ioudaians, who had inherited much of the secret teachings of the Chaldæans, without having preserved the inner meanings. Iêsous is therefore represented as reproaching them in *Luke* xi. 52, saying: "You have taken away the key of the Gnôsis [the arcane wisdom] ; you yourselves have not entered, and those about to enter you have prevented."

[2] Gr. *baptizein*, to dip repeatedly, to wash, to cleanse. There are four lustrations: in *water*, the purification of the material body through psychic (magnetic) action; in *air*, the purification of the psychic body by the action of the vital electricity (*pneuma*); in *fire*, the purification of the Air-body (*sôma pneumatikon*) ; and in *blood*, the purification of the Fire-body in the life-force of the planet ; the spheres of purification being placed, symbolically, in the Moon and the Sun. Thus the followers of Mani represented the Moon and the Sun as two ships by which the soul journeyed to the world of Light. In the lunar boat it was lustrated in "the good water of the Moon," which removed all gross impurities, when it was transferred to the solar boat, where "the good fire of the Sun " consumed all inner impurities, leaving it bright and luminous. (Augustine, *De Hæres.* c. 46; also Epiphanius and others.)

[3] Iôannês, representing the lunar (psychic) man, can only purify through the magnetic force. This subtile ether permeating the body gradually eliminates the grosser elements and clears the channels for the action of the vital

stands one whom *you* do not know, who is
coming behind me, of whom *I* am not deserv-
ing to untie the thong of his sandal."

These [events] took place in Bêthania,[1] on
the other side of the Iordanos, where Iôannês
was lustrating.

On the morrow he sees Iêsous coming toward
him, and says:

"See; [here is] the Lamb of The God, who
takes away the sin[2] of the world. This

electric fire, which then takes the place of the water, or
magnetic nerve-fluid.

[1] Bêthania was a village near Hierousalêm. Origen and
others admit that there was no Bêthania on the east bank
of the Iordanos. Many later manuscripts read "Bêth-
abara." There are a number of such inaccuracies in this
Evangel, with others relating to chronology and Ioudaian
customs, from which it is clear that the author was not a
Ioudaian. Apparently he was not even acquainted with
the Hebrew language. The peculiarly crabbed style of
his Greek, which is curiously out of keeping with the
classic beauty of the narrative, with its vivid picturing,
purity, and dramatic strength, shows that he was writing
in an acquired language; while the literary form, especially
in the dialogues, is distinctly Syrian. Evidently the author
was himself from "the other side of the Iordanos," and a
native of Syria.

[2] Gr. *hamartia*, missing the mark, error, failure, sin. The
kosmos, or material world, is but an imperfect manifestation of the archetypal world. Physical man is a failure
through the "fall into generation"—the separation into
the sexes.

[Anointed] is he of whom *I* said, ' Behind me comes a man who has come to be in front of me, for he was my First.'[1] And *I* did not know him, but that he might shine forth to Israêl, for this [reason] *I* came, lustrating in Water."

And Iôannês bore witness, saying :

"*I* have seen the Breath[2] coming down like a dove out of the Sky,[3] and it abode upon him. And *I* did not know him ; but he who sent me to lustrate in Water, *he* said to me, ' Upon

[1] Or "prototype." Colloquially, the phrase would mean " first of me "— that is, " first in regard to me."

[2] Gr. *pneuma*, the air we breathe, breath ; the magnetic breath or " breath of life " ; spirit. Psycho-physiologically, the vital principle in each of the three bodies. Kosmically, it is the Ether of Space, the " Heavenly Mother."

[3] Gr. *ouranos*, visible Space, the vault of the sky ; the abode of the Gods, beyond the sky-vault. While " heaven " is not situated in the Sky, it nevertheless corresponds, as *subjective* Space, to the outer, visible, or *objective* Space, since the " things seen " are manifestations of the " things unseen," and ancient philosophy never lost sight of the analogy and the relation of the inferior to the superior worlds. Thus Paulos (*Phil.* ii. 10) speaks of " beings in the Sky (*epouranioi*), and beings on the Earth, and subterranean beings." And the term *hoi epouranioi* is synonymous with *hoi theoi*, " the Gods "— the souls of men. Psycho-physiologically, *ouranos* is the brain, the seven centres of which correspond to the seven sidereal worlds or " heavens." The " Breath coming down like a dove out of the Sky " is descriptive of the magnetic irradiation from the brain, which forms a luminous appearance about the spiritually purified man.

whom you may have seen the Breath coming
down, and abiding upon him, this [Anointed]
is he who lustrates in the pure [1] Breath.' And
I HAVE seen, and have borne witness that this
[Anointed] is the Son of The God."

On the morrow again stood Iôannês, and two
of his pupils; and having gazed at Iêsous walk-
ing, he says:
"See; [here is] the Lamb of The God."
And the two pupils heard him speaking,[2] and
they went along after Iêsous; and Iêsous, hav-
ing turned about, and seeing them coming
along after him, says to them:
"What do you seek?"
And they said to him:
"*Rabbi*" (which means, being interpreted,
Teacher), "where do y o u abide?"
He says to them:
"Come and see."
They came, therefore, and saw where he
abides, and they abode with him that day; it
was about the tenth hour. Andreas, the

[1] Gr. *hagios,* pure; consecrated to the Gods, sacred. In
Thess. iv. 3–7, purification (*hagiasmos*) is contrasted with
sexual impurity and the sensual desires.

[2] Gr. *lalein,* to make a prattling, babbling sound (usually
of animals); to babble, to talk; in *New Testament* usage,
to declare secrets, to reveal what has been learned psychically or spiritually, to speak under inspiration or from a
controlling influence.

brother of Simôn Petros, was one of those two who heard from Iôannês, and went along after him. This [pupil] first finds his own brother Simôn, and says to him:

" We have found the *Messias* " (which is, being interpreted, Anointed).

He led him to Iêsous. Iêsous, having gazed at him, said:

" Y o u are Simôn, the son of Iônas; y o u shall be named *Kêphas* " (which is interpreted Petros) [1]

On the morrow he wished to go out into Galilaia; and he finds Philippos, and says to him:

" Come with me "

[1] Gr. *petros*, a rock, a boulder; Chaldaic, *kêphas*, a rock. Here, a word-play upon the Semitic *peter*, meaning an interpreter, illuminator, the hierophant in the Mysteries being so called. The arcane rites were celebrated in caves and rock-temples; the stone receptacle in which the sacred symbols were kept was called the *petrôma*, the same name being given to the double stone tablet from which the hierophant expounded (hence the fable, which rests on a mere pun, about Petros being in Rome). Many words referring to the oracles are derived from *petra* (rock); thus Pataros, the son of the Oracle-God Apollôn, was said to have founded the Oracle-city of Patara. Philo Judæus calls the Logos a Rock; and Paulos (I. *Cor.* x. 1–4) gives a purely mystical interpretation of the myth of the " Rock in the desert ": " Our Fathers were all under the Cloud, and all passed through the Sea, and all were lustrated into

Now, Philippos was from Bêthsaida, out of the city of Andreas and Petros. Philippos finds Nathanaêl, and says to him:

"[The one] whom Môsês described in the Law, and [whom] the Seers [foretold], we have found — Iêsous of Nazareth, the son of Iôsêph."

And Nathanaêl said to him:

"Out of Nazareth can there be anything good?"

Philippos says to him:

"Come and see."

Iêsous saw Nathanaêl coming to him, and he says about him:

"See; [this is] an Israêlite truly, in whom there is no deceit."

Nathanaêl says to him:

"From what source do y o u have knowledge of me?"

Môsês in the Cloud and in the Sea; and all ate the same pneumatic food and drank the same pneumatic drink, for they drank from a pneumatic Rock accompanying them, and that Rock was the Anointed." Psycho-physiologically, the rock is the " philosopher's stone," the " third eye" of the Seer, as clearly shown in *Matt.* xvi. 18, 19 : "*Y o u* are a Rock (*Petros*), and on this rock (*petra*) I will build my Society, and the gates of Hadês shall not prevail against it. And I shall give y o u the keys of the Ruling of the Skies." The " gates of Hadês " are the generative powers, as opposed to the " gate (or door) of Iêsous " (see note 2, p. 150) ; and the " Ruling of the Skies " (*basileia tôn ouranôn*) is the controlling of the seven brain-centres by the Breath (*pneuma*), and thus attaining seership on the sidereal planes.

Iêsous answered and said to him:

"Before Philippos called y o u, when y o u were [yet] under the fig-tree,[1] I saw y o u."

Nathanaêl answered and says to him:

"*Rabbi, y o u* are the Son of The God; *y o u* are the Ruler[2] of Israêl."

Iêsous answered and said to him:

"Because I *said* to y o u that I saw y o u hidden beneath the fig-tree, do y o u believe [it]? You shall *see* greater [things] than these!" And he says to him: "Amên, Amên,[3] I say to you, From now on you shall see the Sky opened, and the Messengers[4] of The God

---

[1] That is, "before y o u were born." The fig is a symbol of the matrix; and its three-lobed leaf represents the creative triad.

[2] Gr. *basileus*, one having authority; a king by right of spiritual knowledge, as opposed to *turannos*, one who usurps authority by physical force; a lord, master, householder. The second of the nine Athenian Archons was called Basileus, and had charge of the religious rites.

[3] See note 4, p. 76. The Amên is used before important declarations to awaken the mind of the listener, the magical vibrations of sound acting upon the brain and making it more receptive. It is also employed in arousing to action the vital electric force, thereby inducing the trance state. It is the mystical "name" of the Christos (II. *Cor.* i. 20; *Rev.* iii. 14). The repetition, "Amên, Amên," occurs only in this *Evangel*.

[4] Gr. *angelos*, a courier, envoy, messenger; a spiritual being or intelligent force. The seven Archangels are the spirits of the seven sacred planets, the hierarchies of formative forces acting upon the kosmos. Here, Petros is the

going up and coming down upon the Son of the Man."

And on the third day a marriage[1] took place in Kana of Galilaia, and the mother of Iêsous was there; and Iêsous was invited,[2] and his pupils also, to the marriage. And the wine having fallen short, the mother of Iêsous says to him:

"They have no wine."

Iêsous says to her:

"What [is that] to me and to y o u, [good] woman[3]? My hour has not yet come."

"third eye" (the "philosopher's stone"), and the Messengers are the seven prismatic colors incessantly playing about it when awakened, each color corresponding to one of the seven Breaths. In a wider sense, these Messengers are the souls of men, and their "going up and coming down" relates to the cycle of incarnations.

[1] Gr. *gamos*, a wedding; union of the sexes; one of the arcane rites; the union of positive and negative forces, the blending of superior and lower natures. Here, the marriage stands for the action of the dual magnetic force in wakening the "third eye," in the attainment of seership; but at this stage of the allegory it refers only to one of those rare visions that come long before the permanent state of illumination is reached.

[2] Literally, "was called."

[3] The Greek word is used as a term of respect, as in Xenophon (*Cyr.* v. 1): "The elder said to the queen, 'Be of good cheer, woman.'" It corresponds to the French *Madame* when thus used in the vocative, though it is rarely placed at the beginning of a sentence when so employed.

His mother says to the waiters [1]:

"Whatever he may say to you, that do."

Now, there were six stone water-jars there, placed according to the Ioudaians' custom of cleansing, holding two or three measures [2] apiece. Iêsous says to them:

"Fill the water-jars with water."

And they filled them to the brim. And he says to them:

"Draw now, and bring [it] to the banquet-master." [3]

And they brought [it]. Now, when the banquet-master had tasted the water which had become wine — and he did not know from what source it was, but the waiters knew, who had drawn the water — he, the banquet-master, addresses the bridegroom, and says to him:

"Usually a man [4] sets on the good wine first, and when [the guests] have become tipsy,[5] then

[1] Gr. *diakonos*, one who waits on or serves another, but not necessarily a menial, or "servant."

[2] Gr. *metrêtês*, a liquid measure, the Roman *amphora*, of nine gallons; but it is uncertain whether the word is used here for precisely that measure. Nor is it of any consequence in the allegory; for the six water-jars stand for the six brain-centres, the water being the psychic forces, and the "wine" being the electric fire in the highest centre.

[3] Gr. *architriklinos*, president of the *triclinium*, or dining-room having three couches.

[4] In the English idiom, "men generally."

[5] Gr. *methuskesthai*, to get drunk, to become intoxicated.

that which is weaker; *y o u* have kept the good
wine till now."

This first of the signs[1] Iêsous did in Kana of
Galilaia; and he made his Radiance shine forth,
and his pupils believed in him.

After this [event], he went down to Kapharnaum, himself and his mother, and his brothers
and his pupils; and there they abode for not
many days. And the "Passing-over"[2] of the
Ioudaians was near; and Iêsous went up to
Hierousalêm, and he found in the temple-

[1] Gr. *sêmeion*, distinctive mark, token, password; symbol; sign from the Gods, omen, portent; constellation; a
transmutation of one element into another, a magical feat
performed through knowledge of the correlations of the
elements. The signs are the geometrical principles of
Form in the sidereal world, whence the grouping of the
atoms to constitute the various elements, the rates of vibration which manifest in the world of the senses as color,
sound, etc. They are the types, models, or ideals after
which the forces (*dunameis*) fashion all things in the objective world; in the sidereal body (*sôma pneumatikon*),
which is atomic but non-molecular, they are the force-
centres; in ceremonial magic they are symbols and
thaumaturgical feats.

[2] Gr. *pascha* (from Heb. *pesach*), one of the three principal
Ioudaian festivals; it was held on the fourteenth day of the
month Nisan, and followed on the fifteenth by the seven-
days festival of the full-moon, that being the first full-
moon of spring. A lamb was sacrificed, as the festival re-
lated to the passing-over of the Sun into the sign Aries,
the Ram having been replaced as a symbol by the Lamb.

courts[1] those who were selling oxen and sheep and doves, and the money-changers[2] sitting [at their tables]   And having made a scourge of ropes, he drove all [the cattle] out of the temple-courts, alike the sheep and the oxen[3]; and he poured out the small coin of the money-brokers,[4] and overturned their tables; and to those who were selling the doves he said:

"Take these [things] hence. Make not my Father's house a house of merchandise."

Then his pupils called to mind that it is written, "The zeal of y o u r house will eat me up."[5]

The Ioudaians, therefore, answered and said to him:

"What sign do y o u show us, in that y o u do these [things] ? "

Iêsous answered and said to them:

"Demolish this temple,[6] and in three days I will raise it [again]."

---

[1] Gr. *hieros*, the temple-enclosure, as distinguished from *naos*, the temple proper.

[2] Gr. *kermatistês*, one who changes small pieces of money (from *kerma*, a small coin).

[3] The Sinaitic reads, "and having found . . . he made," etc., and " he cast out of the temple-courts the sheep and the oxen."

[4] Gr. *kollubistês* (from *kollubos*, a small gold coin; a small gold weight; rate of foreign exchange).

[5] *Ps.* lxix. 9.

[6] Gr. *naos*, a house, especially the dwelling of a God, a temple ; the inmost recess of a temple.

The Ioudaians, therefore, said:

"Forty-six years has this temple been in building, and will *y o u* raise it in three days?"

But *he* was speaking about the temple of his *body*. When, therefore, he was raised from among the dead ones,[1] his pupils called to mind that he had uttered this [prediction], and they had faith in the writing[2] and in the saying[3] which Iêsous had spoken.

Now, while he was in Hierousalêm at the "Passing-over," the festival, many [persons] trusted in his Name, beholding the signs[4] which he made. But Iêsous himself was not for entrusting himself to *them*, through his own knowledge of them all, and because he had no need that any one should bear witness about the Man; for he himself knew what was in the Man.[5]

[1] Gr. *nekros*, a dead human body, a dead man; in the plural (*hoi nekroi*), souls in the Under-world (*hadês*). The term is also applied to men who live solely in the world of the senses, and are dead to spiritual things.

[2] Gr. *graphê*, anything drawn, painted, or written. Here, the sacred scrolls of the Ioudaians.

[3] Gr. *logos*, a statement, an oracular saying with a hidden meaning. See note 2, p. 71.

[4] Or, "his signs," in the Greek idiom.

[5] That is, many saw psychically the luminous appearances in the magnetic Radiance enveloping him, and thereby knew him to be the Spiritual Teacher for the coming cycle (the "Man"); but he did not openly declare himself to them. By a play on the meanings of the verb

Now, there was a man of the Pharisaians —
Nikodêmos [was] his name — a leader[1] of the
Ioudaians. This [man] came to him by night
and said:

"*Rabbi*, we know that y o u have come from a
God as a Teacher; for no one can do these signs
which you do unless The God is with him."

Iêsous answered and said to him:

"Amên, Amên, I say to you, If any one be
not born from above[2] he can not see the
Realm[3] of The God."

---

pisteuein, "to trust" and "to entrust," impossible to be
rendered literally in English, it is implied that their intuitive certainty came spontaneously to them, and was not
initiated or inspired by Iêsous from his higher knowledge.

[1] Gr. *archôn*, chief, captain; king; magistrate.

[2] Gr. *anôthen*, from above; from the first, over again
(but very rarely used in this sense). The sidereal body is
said to be "born from above," that is, from the brain-
centres; the physical body being "born from below."
The Immortals are *hoi anô*, "those above," as distinguished
from the mortals, who are *hoi katô*, "those below," and *hoi
nekroi*, "the dead ones," meaning those incarnated in the
dead forms (physical bodies), and also those in the nether-
world or region of "ghosts" — men in the psychic body,
whether the physical body is dead or only in the sleeping
state. Nikodêmos, however, takes the word *anôthen* in the
sense "over again," thus betraying his ignorance. Such
word-plays are common in this *Evangel;* and Iêsous is usually represented as speaking in a mystical way, while his
listeners are made to appear very materialistic, under-
standing his words only in a crudely literal sense.

[3] Gr. *basileia*, royal power, dominion, rule; a kingdom.

Nikodêmos says to him:

"How can a man be *born* when he is old? Into the womb of his mother can he enter a second time and be born?"

Iêsous answered:

"Amên, Amên, I say to you, If any one be not born of Water and of Breath, he can not enter into the Realm of The God. That which has been born from the flesh is flesh, and that which has been born from the Breath is Breath. Do not wonder because I said to you, You have to be born from above. The Breath breathes where it wills, and you hear its voice[1]; but you do not know whence it comes and where it goes. So is every one who has been born from the Breath."[2]

Nikodêmos answered and said to him:

"How can these [things] be brought about?"

Iêsous answered and said to him:

---

[1] Gr. *phônê*, a tone, articulate sound; a vowel sound (as opposed to that of consonants); voice, speech. The Breath has seven sounds (the "seven vowels" of the Gnostics), corresponding mystically to the seven planes of the sidereal world. These sounds are heard in succession by the mystic as the Breath awakens the seven brain-centres. They are also called "trumpet-calls" (*salpinges*) in the *New Testament*, the seventh heralding the new-birth or "awakening of the dead ones" (I. *Cor.* xv. 52; *Rev.* xi. 15–xii. 1, 2).

[2] Alluding to the mysterious coming and going of the Initiate in his Fire-body, or *sôma pneumatikon.*

" Are *y o u* the Teacher of Israêl and do not know these [things]? Amên, Amên, I say to you, That which we know, we speak, and that which we have seen, we bear witness to; and our witness you do not receive. If I told you the [Mysteries] of the Earth,[1] and you did not believe [me], how, if I tell you the [Mysteries] of the Sky, will you believe [me]? And no one has gone up into the Sky, unless he who came down out of the Sky—the Son of the Man, he who *is*[2] in the Sky. And as Môsês raised on high the Snake in the desert, so shall the Son of the Man have to be raised on high[3] that every one who believes in him may not die, but have On-going[4] Life. For The God so loved the world

[1] Earth (*gaia*) is the lowest of the four subtile elements, and is the material aspect of the World-Soul; Sky (*ouranos*, the expanse of air) being the spiritual aspect. Gaia is therefore represented as the bride of Ouranos, the two standing for the psychic and spiritual worlds respectively. The "things of the Earth" (*ta epigaia*) are psychic; the "things of the Sky" (*ta epourania*), sidereal.

[2] That is, whose real being is always in the higher realm, even when manifesting in the lower worlds. Even when incarnate, the "Son of The God"—the true Self of man—still exists independently, as before, in the infinitudes of Space.

[3] The snake on the cross symbolizes the spiral action of the Breath coiling about the cross in the brain.

[4] Gr. *aiôn*, a period of time; a manifestation of life in time, period of evolution; lifetime (from the Sanskrit root *i*, "to go," the concept of time being inseparable from that

that he gave his Son, the Self-born, that every
one who believes in him may not die, but have
On-going Life. For The God did not send his
Son into the *world* that he might separate[1] the
world, but that through him the world might
be saved.[2] He who believes in him is not separated; but he who does not believe has been
separated already, in that he has not believed
in the Name of the Self-born Son of The God.
And this separating is because the Light has
come into the world, and the Men loved rather
the Darkness than the Light, for their works[3]

of motion, and time being measured by the motion of the
heavenly bodies in space). The God alone is Eternal or
Boundless Duration; everything manifested has limits in
time and space. The highest *aiôn* is the lifetime of the
manifested Universe, considered as a conscious divine
being; and each evolutionary cycle — as the lifetime of
the planetary system, of the earth, of a human race — is
also an *aiôn* and collectively a being. The sidereal body
(*sôma pneumatikon*) of man endures throughout the life-cycle
of the kosmos, and so after the mystic birth "from
above" his consciousness is continuous throughout all the
lesser cycles of reincarnations, racial periods, etc., which
constitute the great On-going or Day of the Gods.

[1] Gr. *krinein*, to separate, put asunder; to pick out,
choose, distinguish; to decide, determine, judge.

[2] Gr. *sôzesthai*, to be kept alive, preserved, saved; to es-
cape, get well; frequently used in the *New Testament* in the
sense of "making whole," "healing."

[3] Gr. *ergon*, deed, work, action; employment; mental
effort. In *New Testament* terminology, works (*erga*) are the
labors of purification, by which the soul regains its freedom.

were useless.[1] For every one who practises worthless [2] [things] hates the Light, and does not come to the Light, that his works may not be brought to proof. But he who does the Truth comes to the Light, that *his* works may shine forth, for they have been accomplished in a God." [3]

After these [things] Iêsous and his pupils came into the Ioudaian country, and there he made a stay with them, and was lustrating.

[1] Gr. *ponêros*, unlucky, sorry, good-for-nothing; bad, knavish.

[2] Gr. *phaulos*, paltry, mean, trifling; shabby, ugly; easy. The useless and worthless works are those that are performed from ignoble motives or for selfish ends, and do not make for spiritual progress. The many (*hoi polloi*) who lead thoughtless lives, absorbed in the objects of the senses, and having no definite purpose, no knowledge of the realities of the inner life, are called "the useless ones" (*hoi ponêroi*), "the worthless ones" (*hoi phauloi*), and even "the dead ones" (*hoi nekroi*), as contrasted with "the wise" (*hoi sophoi*) and "the perfect" (*hoi teleioi*), the purified men and the Initiates, who take conscious control of the forces of evolution and become co-workers with the divine principle in Nature. The "useless ones" are simply the immature souls, of few incarnations and little experience; and the sense of positive "evil" does not attach to the term, nor is it one of reproach.

[3] That is, they are in harmony with the energies of the World-Soul, or God of this planet. "A God" (*theos* without the article), in the *New Testament*, is usually applied to the Logos, as distinguished from The God.

And there was Iôannês also, lustrating in Ai-
nôn, near Salêm, for there were many waters
there, and [people] were coming and being
lustrated. For Iôannês had not yet been cast
into the prison. There arose then a questioning on the part of the pupils of Iôannês with a
Ioudaian, about cleansing[1]; and they came to
Iôannês and said to him:

"*Rabbi*, he who was with y o u on the other
side of the Iordanos, as to whom *y o u* have
borne witness — see, *he* is lustrating, and all
are coming to him."

Iôannês answered and said:

"A man can not receive anything unless it
be given him from the Sky. *You* yourselves
bear me witness that I said, '*I* am not the
Anointed,' but that I have been sent in advance
of him. He who has the bride is the bridegroom; but the friend of the bridegroom, who
stands and hears him, rejoices with joy because

[1] Gr. *katharismos*, washing, purging; expiatory sacrifice.
This washing was the lowest step in the telestic rites, as in
the ceremonies at Eleusis, where on the second day the
Initiates of the lowest degree (*mustai*) purified themselves
by bathing in the sea. In the Eleusinia the superficial
nature of such purification was symbolized by washing a
hog, which on being released would straightway return to
wallowing in the mire. There is a reference to this, apparently, in II. *Pet.* ii. 22: "It has befallen them according to the true proverb, 'The dog returns to his own
vomit, and the washed hog to wallowing in the mire.'"

of the bridegroom's voice. Therefore this joy of mine has been made full. It is for *him* to go on increasing, and for *me* to be ever getting less.[1] He who comes from above [2] is up above all; he who is from the Earth is of the Earth, and of the Earth he speaks.[3] He who comes from the Sky is up above all, and what he has seen and heard, to this [revelation] he bears witness, and no one [4] receives his witness. He who *does* receive his witness has sealed [it] up, because The God is true.[5] For he whom The God has sent speaks the words [6] of The God; for not by measure does The God give the Breath. The Father loves the Son, and has given all [things] into his hand. He who believes in the Son has On-going Life; but he who refuses obedience to [7] the Son

[1] The psychic (lunar) nature must be superseded by the spiritual (solar) nature.

[2] Gr. *anôthen*. See note 2, p. 94.

[3] Referring to psychic trance-speaking. In the English idiom, "As he is of the Earth, so he speaks of the Earth." See note 2, p. 85.

[4] That is, no one of the profane, the "useless ones."

[5] Gr. *alêthês*, real, as opposed to the apparent. The arcane truths are not revealed in the psychic world (*gaia*). See note 1, p. 78.

[6] Gr. *rhêma*, that which is uttered or spoken; a vocal sound, word; a sentence; speech. Here, the Oracles received under the influence of the Breath.

[7] Or, "mistrusts," "disbelieves." The Sinaitic reads, "does not have Life."

shall not see Life, but the Wrath[1] of The God
remains on him."

When, therefore, the Master knew that the
Pharisaians had heard that Iêsous was making
and lustrating more pupils than Iôannês — although Iêsous himself did not lustrate, but his
pupils [did] — he gave up Ioudaia and went
away again into Galilaia, and he had to pass
through Samareia. He comes, therefore, to a
city of Samareia called Sychar, near the plot
of ground which Iakôb gave to Iôsêph, his
son.[2] And it was there that Iakôb's spring[3]
was. Iêsous, therefore, having become tired
from the journey, sat down, just as he was, by
the spring; it was about the sixth hour. There
comes a woman from Samareia to draw water.
Iêsous says to her:

[1] Gr. *orgê*, violent passion, frenzy, anger. In the terminology of the *New Testament* it stands for the psychic fire,
the destructive force inherent in the material aspect of the
World-Soul (*gaia*). Its nature is clearly set forth by
Paulos (*Eph.* v. 5, 6): "No fornicator, or impure man, or
lascivious man who is a worshipper of Phantoms, has any
inheritance in the Realm of the Anointed, ... for through
these things the Wrath of The God comes on the sons of
disobedience."

[2] *Gen.* xlviii. 21, 22. The allegory of Iôsêph, the *dreamer*
and interpreter of *dreams*, whose father Iakôb gave him a
"coat of many colors"— the psychic colors of the seven
magnetic Breaths — refers to the seven heart-centres.

[3] Gr. *pêgê*, a spring, fountain; source of a river; well.

"Give me to drink."

For his pupils had gone away to the city to buy provisions. The Samareitan woman, therefore, says to him:

"How is it that *y o u*, who are a Ioudaian, ask of *me* to drink, who am a Samareitan woman ?"

(For the Ioudaians do not have friendly dealings with the Samareitans.)[1] Iêsous answered and said to her:

"If y o u had known the free gift of The God, and who he is that says to y o u, 'Give me to drink,' *y o u* would have asked of him, and he would have given y o u *living* water."

The woman says to him:

"Master, y o u have nothing to draw with, and the well[2] is deep. Whence, then, do y o u have this 'living water'?[3] Surely *y o u* are not a greater [benefactor] than our Father Iakôb, who gave us the well, and himself drank from it, and his sons, and his cattle."[4]

---

[1] This parenthetical sentence is not in the Sinaitic and Beza.

[2] Gr. *phrear*, a well, cistern, reservoir.

[3] As usual in the dialogues in this *Evangel*, Iêsous speaks mystically, and his interlocutor takes his words in an absurdly literal sense. This method of contrasting the spiritual meaning with the materialistic interpretation is constantly used throughout the *Evangel*, and is one of its peculiar features.

[4] Gr. *threma*, that which is fed or reared, a nursling; usually applied to animals, but sometimes to men. Here, it *may* mean "household."

Iêsous answered and said to her:

"Every one who drinks of *this* water will thirst again; but whosoever may drink of the water which *I* will give him shall *not* thirst throughout the On-going, but the water which I will give him shall become a spring of water up-gushing throughout On-going Life."

The woman says to him:

"Master, give me this water, that I may not thirst, nor come here to draw."

Iêsous says to her:

"Go, call y o u r husband, and come here."

The woman answered and said:

"I have no husband."

Iêsous says to her:

"Rightly y o u have said, 'I have no husband.' For y o u have had five husbands, and he whom you have now is not y o u r husband [1]; *this* y o u have said truly [2]!"

The woman says to him:

"Master, I perceive that *y o u* are a Seer. Our fathers worshipped in this hill, and *you* say that in Hierousalêm is the place where one should worship."

Iêsous says to her:

[1] In the present stage of humanity only five of the magnetic colors have been developed; the sixth begins to manifest in the purified psychic.

[2] The word "truly" (*alêthes*) here has an ironical force in the Greek.

"[Good] woman, believe me, for an hour is coming when neither in this hill nor in Hierousalêm will you worship the Father. *You* worship that which you do not know; *we* worship that which we know, for the Salvation [1] is from the Ioudaians. But an hour is coming, and now is, when the true worshippers will worship the Father in Breath and Truth; for the Father also seeks such as his worshippers. The God is Breath, and those who worship him should worship in Breath and Truth."

The woman says to him:

"I know that the *Messias* is coming, who is called Anointed; when *he* shall have come, he will bring back messages [2] about all [things] to us."

Iêsous says to her:

"*I* who am speaking to y o u am he."

And at this [point] his pupils came, and they wondered that he was talking with a woman. Nevertheless no one said, "What do y o u seek?" or, "Why do y o u talk with her?" The woman, therefore, left her water-jar, and went off into the city, and says to the men:

---

[1] Gr. *sôtêria*, a keeping alive, saving; deliverance; safety. See note 2, p. 97.

[2] Gr. *anangellein*, to bring back tidings or messages; to report. The soul, when immersed in matter, is like one in a far country; and the divinely sent Teachers bring to the incarnated souls tidings of their primeval home.

"Come [and] see a man who told me all [things] which I have done. Can it be that this [Seer] is the Anointed ?"

They came forth from the city, and began to come to him. And in the meantime his pupils kept entreating him, saying:

"*Rabbi*, eat !"

But he said to them:

"*I* have food to eat which *you* do not know."

Then the pupils said to one another:

"Can any one have brought him [something] to eat ?"[1]

Iêsous says to them:

"*My* food is that I should do the will of him who sent me, and make perfect[2] *his* work. Do not *you* say that it is yet four months, and the reaping comes? Behold! I say to you, lift up your eyes and view the regions,[3] that they are white for reaping already. He who reaps receives pay, and gathers fruit into On-going

---

[1] See note 3, p. 102.

[2] Gr. *telein*, to bring to fruition, make perfect; to consecrate; to initiate (into the Mysteries). Here, the work is that of self-purification — the telestic labor. The "perfecting-period" (*telos*) was a term for Initiation, the "making-perfect" (*teletê*) being the ceremony of Initiation into the Mysteries, and the "perfect-ones" (*teleioi*) being the Initiates.

[3] Gr. *chôra*, a place, space, land, country, tract. Here, the inner planes of life, ripe with the accumulated experience of past incarnations.

Life, so that both he who sows and he who reaps may rejoice together. For in this [fact] is that true saying,[1] 'One there is who sows, and another one who reaps.' *I* sent you to reap that which *you* have not toiled at; other ones have toiled, and *you* have entered into their toil."

Now, out of that city many of the Samareitans believed in him, through the saying of the woman who bore witness: "He told me all [things] which I have done." The Samareitans, therefore, came to him and urged him to abide with them; and he abode there two days. And many more [people] believed through his saying, and they said to the woman:

"We do not now believe through y o u r witness,[2] for we ourselves have heard [him], and we *know* that this is truly the Saviour[3] of the world — the Anointed."[4]

---

[1] Or, "arcane maxim." The lower self (the psychic nature) is the sower toiling in the material worlds, and the higher self (the spiritual nature) is the reaper; yet at the "perfecting-period" the two become one.

[2] Some manuscripts have "because of y o u r talk."

[3] Gr. *sôtêr*, a saviour, preserver, deliverer; a tutelary God. The title *sôtêr* was commonly applied to Zeus, Apollôn, or any Solar God.

[4] The ingratitude of men in general, their dulness at comprehending spiritual teachings, and their tendency to materialize every metaphysical concept, are mercilessly satirized in this *Evangel;* and the lash is applied un-

Now, after the two days he went out thence
and went away into Galilaia. For Iêsous himself bore witness that a Seer has no honor in
his own country. When, therefore, he came
into Galilaia the Galilaians welcomed him,
having seen all that he did in Hierousalêm at
the festival; for they also came to the festival.
He came again, therefore, to Kana of Galilaia,
where he [had] made the water wine. And
there was a certain Official,[1] whose son was ill in
Kapharnaum. This [man], having heard that
Iêsous had come out of Ioudaia into Galilaia,
went off to him, and urged him to come down
and cure his son, for he was at the point of
dying. Iêsous, therefore, said in reply to him:

"Unless you have seen signs and portents[2]
you will *not* believe!"

sparingly upon the priestly hierarchy for their ignorance
of the sacred Mysteries, their intolerance, fanaticism, and
despotism. Sublime as the *Evangel* is, with its mystical
fervor and tender pathos, it is sadly pensive, and a vein of
satire, almost of cynicism, runs through it all.

[1] Gr. *basilikos*, a courtier, prince, lord. Here, probably
some officer under the Tetrarch of Galilaia.

[2] Gr. *teras*, any unusual thing due to hidden causes, fore-
boding the future, or revealing the will of the Gods, as the
rainbow, a meteor, or any sign in the skies. The word is
used in the *New Testament* only in the plural (*terata*) and
always joined with *sêmeia* (signs) and often with *dunameis*
(forces); for the portents are visible manifestations of the
forces (*dunameis*) emanating from the signs. See note 1,
p. 91.

The Official says in reply to him:

"Master, come down before my little lad dies."

Iêsous says to him:

"Go y o u r way; y o u r son lives."

The man believed in the saying that Iêsous said to him, and went his way. And now, while he was going down, his slaves met him and brought a message, saying:

"Y o u r boy lives."

He inquired of them, therefore, the hour in which he began to get better. And they said to him:

"Yesterday, at the seventh hour, the fever left him."

The father, therefore, knew that [it was] at that hour in which Iêsous said to him, "Y o u r son lives." And he himself believed, and his whole household.

This, again, a second sign,[1] Iêsous did when he had come out of Ioudaia into Galilaia.

After these [things] there was a festival of the Ioudaians, and Iêsous went up to Hierousalêm. Now, there is in Hierousalêm, by the sheep-[gate], a swimming-bath [2] which is called in Hebrew Béthesda, having five porticos.[3] In

---

[1] The Vatican reads, "Now, this is again the second sign."

[2] The Sinaitic reads, "There is at Hierousalêm a bath for sheep."

[3] Gr. stoa, a pillared walk, colonnade, cloister, piazza.

these [porticos] were lying a crowd of those
who were infirm — blind, lame, shrivelled —
waiting for the moving of the water; for a
Messenger, according to a season,[1] went down
into the swimming-bath and stirred up the water; the first, therefore, to step in after the
stirring-up of the water became healed of whatever disease by which he was weighed down.

Now, there was a certain man there who for
thirty-eight years had been in his infirmity.
Iêsous seeing this [man] lying prostrate, and
knowing that he had now been [thus] for a
long time, says to him:

"Do y o u wish to become well?"

The infirm man answered him:

"Master, I have no man, that, when the water
is stirred up, he may put me into the swimming-
bath; but while *I* am coming, some one else goes
down before me."

[1] Gr. *kairos*, a fixed time; a season, as winter, etc. This
passage concerning the Messenger stirring up the water is
rejected as an interpolation by most modern critics, in their
anxiety to repudiate everything magical. But not only is
the evidence of the ancient manuscripts overwhelmingly in
favor of its genuineness, but also the fact that it is *inseparable* from the context proves absolutely that it cannot be
an interpolation, for without it the rest of the narrative is
meaningless. That the sick were there to be healed, and
that the healing took place only when the water was stirred
up by the Messenger, is clearly indicated by the abrupt
question put by Iêsous to the blind man, and by the latter's
reply.

Iêsous says to him:

"Rise, take up y o u r pallet, and walk."

And at once the man became sound, and got up, and took up his pallet, and walked. Now, it was a Sabbath[1] on that day. The Ioudaians, therefore, said to him who had been healed:

"It is a Sabbath — it is not permissible for y o u to take up [and carry] y o u r pallet."

He answered them:

"He who made me well, *he* said to me, 'Take up y o u r pallet, and walk.'"

They asked him, therefore:

"Which is the man who said to y o u, 'Take up y o u r pallet, and walk'?"

But he who had been cured did not know who it was; for Iêsous had slipped out, there being a crowd in the place.

After these [things] Iêsous finds him in the temple-courts, and says to him:

"See; y o u have become sound. Sin no more, lest something worse should befall y o u."

The man went away, and reported to the

---

[1] The seventh day, or day of rest. The Ioudaians had no names for the days of the week, nor did they compute time by weeks. They observed each *seventh* period of time, including the seventh year, as sacred to their tribal God (Saturn), and their sacred day (Saturday) fell on that ascribed to Saturn when the present Christian week was arranged. The observance of Sunday (the day of the Sun) belongs to the Solar cult, and apparently was introduced into Christianity from the Mithraic religion.

Ioudaians that Iêsous was he who had made him sound.[1] And for this [reason] the Ioudaians hounded Iêsous, because he did these [works] on a Sabbath. But Iêsous answered them:

"My Father is working until now, and *I* am working."[2]

For this [reason], therefore, the Ioudaians sought the more to kill him, because he was not only desecrating the Sabbath, but he was also saying The God [was] his own Father — making himself equal to The God. Iêsous answered, therefore, and said to them:

"Amên, Amên, I say to you, The Son can do nothing of himself, unless he sees the Father doing something; for whatever [works] *he* may do, these [works] the Son also does equally. For the Father dearly loves[3] the Son, and shows him all [works] which he himself does; and greater works than these will he show him, that *you* may wonder. For as the Father raises the dead ones[4] and makes [them] alive, so also the Son makes alive those whom he wills. For not even the Father separates any one; but all

---

[1] Apparently being offended because of the rebuke received, and turning ingrate.

[2] Or, "As my Father has been working until now, so *I* also am working."

[3] Gr. *philein*, to love as a friend. See note 1, p. 212.

[4] See note 1, p. 93.

the separating he has given to the Son, that all
may honor the Son even as they honor the
Father. He who does not honor the Son does
not honor the Father who sent him. Amên,
Amên, I say to you, He who hears my saying,
and has faith in him who sent me, has On-going
Life, and does not come into a separating, but
has passed out of the Death[1] into the Life.
Amên, Amên, I say to you, An hour is coming,
and now is, when the dead ones shall hear the
voice of the Son of The God, and those who hear
[it] shall live. For as the Father has Life in himself, so to the Son also he gave to have Life in
himself; and he gave him authority to make a
separating, because he is [the] Son of a Man.
Do not wonder at this [saying], because an
hour is coming in which all those who are in
the tombs shall hear his Voice, and come
forth— those who have done the good [works]
into an Awakening[2] of Life, and those who

[1] Mystically, the physical world is called Death. Thus
in the *Apokalypse* (i. 17, 18) the Initiate says: "*I* am the
First, and the Last, and the Living one, and I became a
dead one [incarnated], yet behold! I am alive throughout
the On-goings of the On-goings, and I have the keys of
Death [the physical world] and of Hadês [the psychic
world]." All things and beings in the material world, the
world of separateness, are under the sway of death; only
in the divine unity of the spiritual world is there true life.

[2] Gr. *anastasis*, a making to stand up (from a suppliant
attitude); awakening, restoration (from the dead). The

have practised the worthless [works] into an
Awakening of separation. *I* can not do anything of myself: as I hear, I separate; and
this separating of mine is well-ordered, because
I do not seek *my* will, but the will of him who
sent me. If *I* bear witness about myself, my
witness is not true; there is another who bears
witness about me, and I know[1] that the witness
which he bears about me is true. *You* have
sent to Iôannês; and he has borne witness to
the Truth. But *I* do not take the witness from

man who has perfected the work of self-purification regains the spiritual state; but the "useless ones" (*hoi
ponêroi*) continue to reincarnate in the physical world of
separateness, this "separateness" signifying not only the
duality of good and evil, but also the duality of the sexes.
For sex is an animal condition, and does not obtain in the
spiritual world, where there is neither death nor birth.
This is clearly set forth by Iêsous in reply to the question
about the childless woman who had been married successively to seven brothers (*Lk.* xx. 34–36): "The sons of
this On-going marry and are given in marriage; but those
accounted worthy to attaining to *that* On-going and that
Awakening from among dead ones neither marry nor are
given in marriage; for they can not die any more, because
they are like the Messengers, and are sons of The God,
being sons of the Awakening." Psycho-physiologically,
the term applies to the restoration of the psychic and
spiritual senses, the organs of which became atrophied (or
"dead") when the human being fell into generation, the
allegorical fall of Adam and Eve (the separation into
sexes), for which they were driven out of Paradise.

[1] The Sinaitic and Beza have, "you know."

a man — yet I say these [things] that *you* may
be saved. *He* was that burning and shining
lamp, and *you* were willing for an hour to become ecstatic [1] in his Light; yet *I* have witness
greater than Iôannês', for the works which the
Father gave me to make perfect — the very
works which I am doing — bear witness about
me, that it is the Father who has sent me. And
the Father who sent me has himself borne witness about me. As yet you have neither at any
time heard his Voice nor seen his Form. And
his Thought [2] you have not abiding in you, because whom *he* sent, in this [witness] *you* have
no faith. You pore over the writings because
you think you have in them On-going Life;
and it is *they* that bear witness about me — yet
you are not willing to come to me that you may
have Life. I do not take Radiance from *men;*
but well I know that *you* have not in yourselves
the Love [3] of The God. *I* have come in my

[1] Gr. *agalliathênai*, to be frenzied with exultation, to be
mad with delight. Here it refers to psychic exaltation, the
frenzy by which the psychic senses are awakened, as in the
Bacchic initiations (*orgia*). The Light of Iôannês is the
psychic (lunar) Light.

[2] Gr. *logos*. See note 2, p. 71.

[3] Gr. *agapê*, love. The word is found only in post-
classical writers, who use it instead of *eros*, the latter word
having become degraded. In the older writers, as Hesiod,
Eros is the first of the Gods, divine Love — the Logos, in
fact — in the sense that *agapê* is used here.

Father's name, and you do not accept me; if another should come in his own name, *him* you will accept. How can *you* have faith, when you take Radiance one from another, and do not seek that Radiance[1] which comes from the Only One[2]? Do not think that I shall accuse you to the Father; he who accuses you to the Father is Môsês, in whom *you* have placed your hope. For if you had faith in Môsês you would have faith in *me*, for it was of *me* that *he* wrote. Now, if you do not believe *his* writings, how will you believe *my* words?"[3]

[1] The word *doxa* is used in this passage with a double meaning: as "glory," and as the *aura*, or magnetic substance; and, in the latter sense, the pure *aura*, or "flesh," of the Logos is contrasted with the *auric* (or magnetic) emanations of men — the latter being considered by ascetics to be defiling and pestilential. Yet the Mosaic Law abounded in regulations concerning psychic hygiene (*Lev.* x. 10; xi.; xii.; xv.; xvii. 10, 11), and that the ancient Hebrews well knew the nature of vital magnetism is shown by the attempt of King David to prolong his life by vampirizing the "fair damsel" Abishag (I. *Kings* i. 1, 2).

[2] The reading in some manuscripts is, "the only God"; but the Vatican has, "Only One," which is clearly more in harmony with the general style of this *Evangel*.

[3] Not having gained wisdom during the cycle of Môsês, they could not understand the arcane teachings of Iêsous, the Teacher for the new cycle. Each of the sidereal months (periods of about 2,155 years) has its spiritual Ruler or Teacher, and constitutes a cycle of instruction; and those who faithfully follow, in each incarnation during that period, the spirit of the teachings of that Saviour are

After these [events] Iêsous went away to the other side of that Sea of Galilaia, the Tiberias. And a great crowd were following him, because they beheld the signs which he made upon those who were sick. And Iêsous went up into the hill, and sat there with his pupils. And the Passing-over, the festival of the Ioudaians, was near. Iêsous, therefore, lifting up his eyes and seeing that a great crowd were coming to him, says to Philippos:

"Where may we buy loaves, that these [people] may eat?"

(Now, he said this to test him, for *he* knew what he intended to do.) Philippos answered him:

"Loaves costing two hundred *denarii*[1] are not enough for them, that each may take a little."

One of the pupils — Andreas, the brother of Simôn Petros — says to him:

"There is a small boy here, who has five barley loaves and two little fishes[2]; but what are *these* [provisions] to so many?"

freed from the bondage of matter — they are "saved." But the Pharisaians followed only the dead-letter of the Mosaic writings. See note 1, p. 82.

[1] About thirty dollars.

[2] The numbers five and two appear also in the *two* hundred denarii and *five* thousand people fed. Astronomically, they refer to the seven sacred planets, of which two (the Sun and the Moon) are not real planets, but substi-

And Iêsous said:

"Make the men recline."

Now, there was much greensward[1] in the place. The men, therefore, reclined — in number about five thousand. Then Iêsous took the loaves, and having returned thanks, distributed [them] to his pupils, and the pupils to those who were reclining, likewise also of the fishes, as much as they wished. And when they were filled, he says to his pupils:

"Collect the fragments that are left over, so that nothing may be lost."

They collected [them] therefore, and filled twelve baskets with fragments from the five barley loaves, which were left over to those who had eaten. The men, therefore, seeing a sign which Iêsous made, said:

"This [magician] is truly the Seer, who comes into the world."

Iêsous, therefore, knowing that perhaps they might come and carry him off, so that they might make him a ruler, withdrew again into the hill, alone by himself. Now, when it came to be evening, his pupils went down to the sea,

tutes for two secret Mystery-planets; and the twelve baskets are the zodiacal signs. Psycho-physiologically, the five manifested and two unmanifested Breaths or principles are meant, as in the story of the woman at the well, but here only as they relate to physical generation.

[1] Gr. *chortos*, grass; a feeding-ground, pasture.

and got into a boat, and were going to the
other side of the sea to Kapharnaum. And
dusk by this time had come on, and Iêsous had
not yet come to them; and the sea, as a great
wind was blowing, began to be stirred. Having,
therefore, rowed about twenty-five or thirty
furlongs, they see Iêsous walking on the sea,
and appearing near the boat; and they were
frightened. But he says to them:

"It is *I;* do not be frightened."

They were willing, therefore, to take him
into the boat — and immediately the boat was
at the land for which they were making.

On the morrow the crowd that was standing
on the other side of the sea saw that there was
no other small-boat there save that one in
which the pupils of Iêsous had embarked, and
that Iêsous had not entered with his pupils
into the boat, but his pupils had gone away
alone. But other small-boats came from Tiberias, near the place where they ate the bread
after the Master had given thanks [over it].
When, therefore, the crowd saw that Iêsous
was not there, nor his pupils, they got into the
boats themselves and came to Kapharnaum,
seeking Iêsous. And having found him on the
other side of the sea, they said to him:

"*Rabbi*, when did y o u get here?"

Iêsous answered and said to them:

"Amên, Amên, I say to you, You seek me, not

because you saw signs, but because you ate of the loaves and were fed full! *Work*—not for the food which perishes, but for that food which abides throughout On-going Life, which the Son of the Man offers you[1]; for this [Son] the Father—The God—has sealed up."[2]

They said to him, therefore:

"What should we do, that we may work the works of The God?"

Iêsous answered and said to them:

"This is the work of The God, that you may believe in him whom *he* sent."

They said to him, therefore:

"Then what sign do *y o u* make, so that we may see [it] and believe y o u? What *do* y o u work at? Our fathers ate the *manna* in the

[1] The Vatican reads, "shall give you."

[2] The loaves and fishes, emblematic of physical generation and the multiplication of bodies in the world of death, are here contrasted with the divine Essence — the Radiance of the Only One — which is the "bread of the Life" in that spiritual world where all beings are sexless, hence "sealed up." This is clearly brought out in I. *Jno*. iii. 8, 9: "He who does this sin is from the Accuser; because the Accuser sins from a First-principle. To this [end] the Son of The God was manifested, that he might undo the works of the Accuser. Any one who has been born from The God does no sin, because his seed (*sperma*) abides in him, and he can not sin, because he has been born from The God." So also v. 18: "Any one who is born from The God does not sin; but he who has been born from The God *keeps himself*, and the useless [function] has no hold on

desert, as it is written, 'Bread out of the Sky he gave them to eat.'"[1]

Iêsous, therefore, said to them:

"Amên, Amên, I say to you, Môsês has not given *you*[2] the bread out of the Sky; but my Father does give you that *true* bread out of the Sky. For the bread of The God is that which comes down out of the Sky and gives Life to the world."

They said to him, therefore:

"Master, give us this bread every time[3]!"

Iêsous said to them:

"*I* am the bread of the *Life;* he who comes to me shall be hungry no more, and he who has faith in me shall be thirsty nevermore. But I said to *you* that though you have even seen me, still you do not have faith. Every-

him." This useless function — the "evil one" or "Devil" of theology — is simply sex; and the misuse of the function is the "sin" against the First-principle, the sacred Breath and creative Fire. In the text, while Iêsous is speaking of the telestic work and the celestial substance of the pneumatic body, his hearers — poverty-stricken and ignorant — think only of obtaining employment and supplying their physical needs.

[1] *Ps.* lxxviii. 24. Here, as is almost invariably the case in the *New Testament*, the quotation is from the *Septuagint*, or Greek version, and not from the Hebrew.

[2] See note 3, p. 115.

[3] Gr. *pantote*, at all times. The word is a homely one (the better writers using *hekastote* or *diapantos*), but it is frequently found in the *New Testament*.

thing which the Father gives me shall come to me; and him who comes to *me* I will *not* throw outside.[1] For I have come down out of the Sky, not that I may do *my* will, but the will of him who sent me. And this is the will of him who sent me, that of everything which he has given me I may not lose any, but should raise it up[2] on the last day.[3] For this is the will of my Father, that every one who sees the Son, and has faith in him, may have On-going Life; and *I* shall raise him up at the last day."

Then the Ioudaians murmured about him, because he said: "*I* am the bread that has come down out of the Sky." And they said: "Is not this [man] Iêsous the son of Iôsêph, whose father and mother *we* know? How, then, does this [man] say, 'I have come down out of the Sky'?"

Iêsous answered and said to them:

"Do not murmur one with another. No one can come to me unless the Father who sent me shall draw him; and I shall raise him up on the last day. It is written in the Seers, 'And

---

[1] Gr. *exô*, on the outside, out of doors; exoteric, as opposed to esoteric (*esô*).

[2] Or, "restore it."

[3] The last incarnation, in which the soul gains its freedom, synthesizes all preceding ones; and the full Initiate regains memory of all his past lives. Nothing is wasted; even the fragments being preserved, as in the preceding allegory.

they shall all be [learners] taught by a God.'[1] Every one who has heard[2] from the Father, and has learned, comes to me. Not that any one has seen the Father, save he who is from The God; this [Son] has seen the Father.[3] Amên, Amên, I say to you, He who has faith in me has On-going Life. *I* am the bread of the Life. Your fathers ate the *manna* in the desert, and they died. This [Son] is the bread which comes down out of the Sky, that any one may eat of it and not die. *I* am that *living* bread that came down out of the Sky. If any one eats of this bread, he shall live throughout the On-going. Aye, and the bread which *I* shall give him is my flesh, which *I* shall give for the Life of the world."[4]

The Ioudaians, therefore, wrangled one with another, saying, "How can this [man] give us his flesh to eat?"

Iêsous, therefore, said to them:

"Amên, Amên, I say to you, Unless you eat the flesh of the Son of the Man, and drink his

[1] *Isa.* liv. 13.

[2] Or, "has listened to [the teaching]."

[3] The Father is the Universal Soul, and the Son the individual soul. The Divine Principle in Nature can be cognized only through the same principle as manifested in man.

[4] The divine Self of man is not fully incarnated in him until he has assimilated its *aura* — the "flesh" of the Logos.

blood, you have not On-going Life[1] in yourselves. He who eats my flesh, and drinks my
blood, has On-going Life, and I shall raise him
up at the last day. For my flesh is truly food,
and my blood is truly drink. He who devours
my flesh and drinks my blood abides in me, as
I do in him.[2] Even as the living Father sent
me, and I live through the Father, so also he
who eats me — *he* also shall live through me.
This is the bread which came down out of the
Sky. Not as your fathers ate and died — he
who eats *this* bread shall live throughout the
On-going."[3]

These [things] he said at a gathering,[4] as he

[1] The Vatican has, " you have not Life"; the Sinaitic,
"the Life."

[2] The Beza has in addition : " Even as the Father in me,
and I in the Father — Amên, Amên, I say to you, Unless
you receive the body of the Son of the Man, as the bread
of the Life, you have not Life in him." There are many
variations in the text throughout this discourse, apparently
due to careless copyists; but none of them materially
affects the meaning.

[3] That the hearers of Iêsous should take literally his oft-
repeated statement about eating his " flesh " and drinking
his " blood" may seem rather a far-fetched satire upon
their stupidity. But, unfortunately, it is almost impossible
to exaggerate the materialistic literalness with which spiritual truths are often regarded; and perhaps no better
instance could be pointed out than the belief of many —
even at the present day — that the bread and wine of the
Eucharist are the actual flesh and blood of Christ.

[4] Gr. *sunagôgê*, an assembling of people, a meeting.

taught at Kapharnaum. Many of his pupils, therefore, hearing him, said:

"Hard is this saying. Who can listen to it?"

But Iêsous, knowing in himself that his pupils were murmuring about this [saying], said to them:

"Does this [saying] trip you up? [What], then, if you should see the Son of the Man going up where he was before? The Breath it is which makes alive; the flesh is of no use in anything. The words which *I* speak to you are Breath and are Life; but there are of *you* some who do not have faith."

For Iêsous knew from a First-principle who they were that did not have faith, and who he was that was about to deliver him up. And he said:

"For this [reason] I have said to you, that no one can come to me, unless it has been given him from my Father."

From this [time], many of his pupils went back to the [things that lay] behind,[1] and no longer walked with him. Iêsous, therefore, said to the Twelve:

---

[1] That is, they went back to the exoteric religion, being unable to understand the esoteric teachings. The metaphor is taken, apparently, from the race-course (*dromos*), and the expression is equivalent to "they fell out of the race." See *Phil.* iii. 13, 14.

" Do *you* also wish to go away ? "

Simôn Petros answered him :

" Master, to what [things] shall we go back ?
Y o u have the words of On-going Life, and *we*
have believed [them], and have known that
y o u are the holy [Anointed] of The God."

Iêsous answered them :

" Did not *I* choose you, the Twelve, and of
you one is an accuser [1] ? "

Now, he was speaking of Ioudas, [the son] of
Simôn Iskariôtês,[2] for this [pupil] was about to
deliver him up, being one of the Twelve.

After these [things] Iêsous walked in Galilaia ; for he was unwilling to walk in Ioudaia,
because the Ioudaians were seeking to kill
him. Now, the Ioudaians' festival, "Tent-
making,"[3] was near. His brothers, therefore,
said to him :

" Quit this place, and go into Ioudaia, so that
y o u r pupils also may see these works of y o u r s

---

[1] Gr. *diabolos*, a slanderer, traducer (from *diaballein*, literally, "to shoot across," traduce ; to accuse secretly). Ioudas secretly preferred false charges against Iêsous, and
misrepresented his teachings to the priests.

[2] In the Greek idiom, "Ioudas Iskariôtês, [the son] of
Simôn."

[3] Gr. *skênopêgia*, fixing the tents. This festival, which
lasted seven days, was celebrated at about the Autumnal
Equinox, and was the greatest of the festivals. See *Deut.*
xvi. 13–17.

which y o u are doing. For no one does anything in secret, and seeks that he should be talked about openly. Since y o u are doing these [works], show yourself plainly to the world."

For not even his own brothers believed in him. Iêsous, therefore, says to them:

"*My* season has not yet come; but *your* season is ready at all times. The world can not hate *you;* but *me* it does hate, because *I* bear witness about it that its works are useless. Go up to the festival yourselves; *I* am not [1] going to *this* festival, because *my* season has not yet been fulfilled."

Having said these [things] to them, he remained in Galilaia. But when his brothers had gone up to the festival, then *he* also went up, not openly, but as if in secret.[2] The Ioudaians, therefore, sought for him at the festival, and said:

"Where is that [man]?"

[1] Porphyrios having twitted the Fathers about this passage, the literal interpretation of which makes Iêsous appear to have changed his mind, the text was subsequently altered to read "not yet" (*oupô*) instead of "not" (*ouk*). The latter is unquestionably the true reading. Iêsous was speaking mystically, referring to the season of his crucifixion; and in this sense his words are not contradicted by his afterwards going up to the exoteric festival.

[2] Presumably using the occult power (*dunamis*) of making himself invisible. See note 3, p. 129.

And there was much murmuring about him among the crowds.[1]   Some said, "He is a good [man]," but others said, "Not so, for he is leading the multitude astray."   No one, however, spoke about him openly, through fear of the Ioudaians.

But when the festival was already half over, Iêsous went up into the temple-courts, and taught.   And the Ioudaians wondered, saying:

"How does this [man] know letters, when he has not learned [them]?"

Iêsous answered and said to them:

"My teaching is not mine, but his who sent me.   If any one wills to do *his* will, he shall have knowledge about the teaching, whether it is from The God, or whether *I* am speaking from myself.   He who speaks from himself seeks his own Radiance; but he who seeks the Radiance of him who sent him, that [man] is true, and there is no dishonesty[2] in him.   Did not Môsês give you the Law? — and not one of you does the Law!   Why are you seeking to kill me?"

The crowd answered:

[1] The knots of talkers, the populace.   The Beza here reads, "common people."

[2] Gr. *adikia*, falsehood, error; as opposed to truth (*alê-theia*).   Incarnated man is "sent" into the world by his own soul, and only by doing the will of that soul can he fulfil the law of being (*dikê*), non-fulfilment of which is *adikia*, "unrighteousness."

"Y o u have a spook'! Who is seeking to
kill y o u?"

Iêsous answered and said to them:

"One work I did, and you are all wonder-
ing. Môsês has given you the circumcision [2] —
not that it is from Môsês, but from the Fathers [3]
— and on a Sabbath you circumcise a man. If
a man receives circumcision on a Sabbath, so
that the Law of Môsês may not be done away
with, are you enraged at *me* because I restored
an entire man to health [4] on a Sabbath? Do

---

[1] Gr. *daimonion* (from *daimôn*, a word that does not occur
in *Iôannês*), a being participating in the Divine Essence or
Universal Soul; an entity intermediate between Gods and
men; a nature-spirit; a ghost or earth-bound soul. Originally the word *daimones* was applied to the souls of the men
of the Golden Age, and to deified heroes; later it came to
signify the souls of the dead in general, and in the *New
Testament* it is usually employed in a bad sense, to denote
ghosts that haunt places and obsess people, the *larvæ* or
"unclean spirits" (*pneumata akatharta*). The word *daimôn*,
in its good sense, is replaced in the *New Testament* by trans-
ferring the meaning to *angelos* ("messenger").

[2] *Lev.* xii. 1–3.

[3] *Gen.* xvii. 9–14.

[4] This is unmistakably the meaning of the Greek, with
which the Latin of the Beza agrees, "*Quod totum hominem
sanum feci in sabbato.*" So also the *Vulgate.* If lawful to
heal part of a man, it would be lawful to heal the whole
man. The rite of circumcision typified, *pars pro toto*,
emancipation from the physical body, as said in *Col.* ii. 11:
"You were circumcised with a circumcision not done with
hands, in the putting off of the body of the flesh, in the

not judge[1] according to appearance, but judge [according to] a just judgment."

Some [persons], therefore, of Hierousalêm said:

"Is not this [man] he whom they are seeking to kill? And see — he is speaking openly, and they say nothing to him. Can it be that the leaders have truly determined that this [man] is the Anointed? Yet this [man] we know, whence he is; but when the Anointed comes, no one knows whence he is."

Iêsous, therefore, cried out loudly, teaching in the temple-courts, and saying:

"You not only know *me*, but you also know whence I am; and I have not come of myself, but he is true who sent me, whom *you* do not know. *I* do know him, because I am from him, and *he* sent me."

They sought, therefore, to take[2] him; and no man laid his hand on him, because his hour had not yet come.[3] But of the multitude many believed in him, and they said:

"When the Anointed comes, will he do more signs than these which this [man] has done?"

circumcision of the Anointed." Here the metaphor is that of stripping off the physical body as if it were a garment.

[1] Gr. *krinein.* See note 1, p. 97.

[2] Gr. *piazein*, to press hard, catch, apprehend.

[3] The easy way in which Iêsous always escaped from his pursuers implies the use of magic. See note 3, p. 143.

The Pharisaians heard the people murmuring these [things] about him, and the archpriests and the Pharisaians sent retainers,[1] so that they might take him. Iêsous, therefore, said:

"Yet a little while I am with you, and I go to him who sent me. You will seek me, and you will not find me; and where *I* am, *you* can not come."

The Ioudaians, therefore, said to themselves:

"Where is this [man] about to go, that *we* shall not find him? Is he about to go to the dispersion[2] of the Hellênes, and to teach the Hellênes? What is this saying which he spoke, 'You will seek me, and you will not find me; and where *I* am, *you* can not come'?"

Now, on the last day, the great [day] of the festival, Iêsous stood and cried out loudly, saying:

"If any one is thirsty, let him come to me, and drink. Whoever believes in me, as the writing has said, 'Out of his belly shall flow rivers of living Water.'"[3]

But this [quotation] he said about the Breath, which those who believed in him were about to

---

[1] Gr. *hupêretês*, a helper, servant, inferior officer.

[2] Gr. *diaspora*, a scattering, dispersion; collectively, the persons dispersed. Here the Ioudaians scattered among the Hellênes (Greeks) are meant.

[3] These words are not found in the *Old Testament*.

receive; for not as yet was there a holy Breath,[1] because Iêsous was not yet made Radiant. Many, therefore, of the people, having heard the saying, said, "This [man] is truly the Seer." Others said, "This [man] is the Anointed." But others said, "Why, surely the Anointed does not come out of Galilaia? Has not the writing said that the Anointed comes of the seed of David,[2] and from Bêthlehem, the village where David was?"[3]

A division, therefore, arose among the people concerning him. And some of them desired to take him; but no one laid his hands on him. The retainers, therefore, came to the archpriests and Pharisaians; and *they* said to them:

"Why did you not bring him?"

The retainers answered:

"Never did a man speak as *this* man [does]."

The Pharisaians, therefore, answered them:

"Surely *you* also have not been led astray? Did any one of the leaders believe in him, or of the Pharisaians? But this crowd, who do not know the Law, they are put under an evil spell."[4]

[1] The text here is corrupt. A preferable but less authoritative reading is, "for the holy Breath was not yet given [to them]." See p. 208.

[2] *Jer.* xxiii. 5, 6.

[3] *Mic.* v. 2.

[4] The priests, learned in the dead-letter of their sacred books, yet destitute of the higher wisdom, consider the people bewitched because they follow the true Teacher.

Nikodêmos — that one of them who had come to him at night — says to them:

" Surely our Law does not judge the [accused] man unless it first hears from him, and knows what he does."[1]

They answered and said to him:

" Possibly *you* also are from Galilaia! Search, and see, that a Seer has *not* arisen out of Galilaia[2]! "

And they went each to his own house; but Iêsous went to the Olive-tree Hill.

Now, at daybreak he came again to the temple-courts, and all the common people[3] came to him; and having sat down, he taught them. But the Recorders[4] and the Pharisaians bring to him a woman caught in adultery, and placing her before all,[5] they say to him:

[1] *Deut.* i. 16, 17.

[2] This is simply an indirect assertion that Iêsous, in *their* opinion, was not a Seer; or the rendering may be, "that out of Galilaia no Seer is to arise," though the latter reading is not that of the older manuscripts. If construed, "no Seer has arisen," the statement would be untrue, as Iônas and other great Seers were of Galilaia. But the priests are sarcastically represented as judging from appearances, being ignorant of the fact that Iêsous was born at Bêthlehem.

[3] Gr. *laos*, the rank and file, the common men.

[4] Gr. *grammateus*, a scribe, secretary; one learned in the Law.

[5] In the Greek idiom, "in the midst."

"Teacher, this woman was caught in the
very act, committing adultery. Now, in the Law
Môsês has commanded us that such should be
stoned.[1] What, therefore, do *y o u* say ?"

Now, they said this to test him, so that they
might be able to bring a charge against him.
But Iêsous, stooping down, wrote on the ground
with his finger[2]; but when they kept asking him,
he lifted himself up and said to them:

"He of you who is *blameless*, let him be the
first to hurl the stone [3] at her."

And again he stooped down and wrote on the
ground. Now, having heard, and being reproached by conscience, they went out one by
one, beginning from those of higher rank,[4] even
to the lowest; and Iêsous alone was left, and
the woman standing before all. Now, Iêsous,
having lifted himself up, and seeing nobody but
the woman, said to her:

"[Good] woman, where are *they*, y o u r prose-

---

[1] *Lev.* **xx.** 10; *Deut.* **xxii.** 22–24.

[2] Symbolizing that evil is inherent in matter, and is therefore impermanent. The soul itself is pure, but the evil im-
pulses of the material body, the animal-self, contaminate it.
See note 1, p. 22.

[3] The custom was for one of the accusers or witnesses to
cast a stone as a signal for the bystanders to begin the
execution.

[4] Gr. *presbuteros*, an elder; a member of the council. So
strong was their pride of position that even in their dis-
comfiture they went out in the order of their rank.

cutors? Has no one passed sentence upon
y o u?"

And she said:

"No one, Master."

And Iêsous said to her:

"Neither do *I* pass sentence upon y o u. Go
y o u r way, and sin no more."[1]

Again, therefore, Iêsous spoke to them, saying:

"*I* am the Light of the world; he who goes
with *me* shall not at all walk in the Darkness,
but shall have the Light of the Life."

The Pharisaians, therefore, said to him:

"*Y o u* are bearing witness about yourself;
y o u r witness is not true."

---

[1] Although the story of the woman taken in adultery has
been rejected as spurious by a majority of the critics, a
more careful weighing of the evidence will conclusively
establish its authenticity; for everything goes to show
that its exclusion from some of the manuscripts was due
solely to the fanaticism of churchmen of the stamp of the
"elders" upon whom it is such a stinging satire. Its morality
was too broad for their narrow code. A majority of about
300 manuscripts, including some of the more ancient ones,
are in favor of the passage; and the fact that many of the
others leave a space for it, or show erasures or torn pages,
shows that the text was unscrupulously mutilated by bigoted
moral critics. It has been urged against its authenticity
that it interrupts the course of the narrative; that it is in
a different style from the rest of the *Evangel*, containing
words and phrases not elsewhere found, and making a different use of particles; and that it has an unparalleled

Iêsous answered and said to them :

"Even if *I* do bear witness about myself, my witness is true, because I know whence I came and where I am going; but *you* do not know whence I come, or where I am going. *You* judge according to the flesh; *I* judge no one. And even if *I* do judge, this judgment of mine is true, because I am not alone, but *I* and the Father who sent me [judge]; and it has also been written in your own Law that two men's witness is true.[1] *I* am one who bears witness about myself, and the Father who sent me bears witness about *me*."

They said to him, therefore :

"Where is y o u r Father ? "

variety of readings. On the contrary, it is an integral part of the narrative, for the expurgated portion begins with the words, " And they went each to his own house," and the sentences immediately preceding and following the omitted passage do not form a sequence, while the sentences directly following apply to it with wonderful clearness and beauty : "I am the Light," says Iêsous (that Light of conscience which had reproached the hearts of the accusers) ; and again, " *You* judge according to the flesh; *I* judge no one." Also the style is identical with that of the whole *Evangel*, and the particles are numerically the same—a strong point in its favor, as the writer is peculiarly sparing in the use of particles; nor is there a greater variety of readings than in some other passages. Indeed, it is curious that any fair-minded critic should ever have seriously questioned the genuineness of the passage.

[1] *Deut.* xix. 15.

Iêsous answered:

" You neither know *me* nor my *Father;* if you knew *me*, you would know my *Father* also."

These words he spoke in the treasury,[1] as he taught in the temple-courts, and no one took him, because his hour had not yet come. Again, therefore, he said to them:

"*I* am going away; and you will seek me, and you will die in your sin. Where *I* am going, *you* can not come."

The Ioudaians, therefore, said:

" Surely he will not kill himself, that he says, ' Where *I* am going, *you* can not come '!"

And he said to them:

" *You* are of those below, *I* am of those above[2]; *you* are of this world, *I* am not of this world. Therefore I said to you that you will die in your sins; for unless you shall believe that *I Am*,[3] you *will* die in your sins."

They said to him, therefore:

" Who *are* ʏ ᴏ ᴜ ? "

And Iêsous said to them:

" And wherefore do I speak to *you* of that

[1] Gr. *gazophulakion*, treasure-house.

[2] That is, " *You* are of the Mortals, *I* am of the Immortals." See note 2, p. 94.

[3] Immortality is gained only through the identification of one's self with the changeless inner consciousness, which is beyond the illusions of Time and the perishable objects of the senses.

First-principle[1] *?* Many [things] I can speak about you, and judge; but he who sent me is true, and *these* [words], which *I* have heard from him, I say to the world."

They did not perceive that he was speaking to them of the Father. Therefore, Iêsous said to them:

"When you have raised on high the Son of the Man, then you will know that *I Am*, and [that] I do nothing of myself, but I speak these [things] even as my Father taught me. And he who sent me is with me; the Father has not left me alone by myself, because I do every time the [works] that are acceptable to him."

While he was speaking these [words], many [hearers] believed in him. Iêsous, therefore, said to the Ioudaians who had believed in him:

"If *you* abide in this saying of mine, you are truly my pupils; and you shall know the Truth, and the Truth shall set you free."[2]

[1] The *logos* and the *archê* are one. See notes 1 and 2, p. 71.

[2] That is, free from the "wheel of birth," or cycle of reincarnations. This freedom comes only through the merging of the individual consciousness in the eternal consciousness of the Son or Logos, the "I Am." Iêsous, as the Logos, is the Saviour and the Deliverer — titles which were also given to Zeus and the other Solar Gods. Sin is the cause of bondage, and in the *Epistle of James* (iii. 6) evil speech is said to be that which "inflames the

They answered him:

"We are Abraham's seed, and never yet have been slaves[1] to any one. How is it *you* say, 'You shall become freemen'?"

Iêsous answered them:

"Amên, Amên, I say to you, *Every one* who commits a sin is a slave to sin.[2] Now, the slave does not abide in the house throughout the On-going; the Son does abide throughout the On-going. If, therefore, the Son shall set you free, you shall be 'freemen' indeed.[3] I

wheel of birth" — apparently alluding to the myth of Ixion, who was bound to a flaming wheel as a punishment for his sins. Ixion, cast out of heaven, is the soul fallen into generation, and bound to the fiery wheel of the animal passions.

[1] Presumably the speakers, taking the mystical words of Iêsous literally, of course, were thinking of chattel slavery, and not of national subjugation; otherwise their boast could not be reconciled with the facts of history, as the Ioudaians were at that time in subjection to the Romans, having previously been in slavery under the Egyptians, Assyrians, and Babylonians.

[2] Or, "a slave to that sin." The wording leaves it uncertain whether sin in the abstract or some particular sin is meant. Yet the former is doubtless intended, since it is contrasted with the Truth. Illusion, the mistaking of the False for the True, is the source of sin, and pertains to the material world, while Truth is of the spiritual world.

[3] The metaphor is drawn from the Roman system of enfranchising slaves and making them legally freemen (*liberti*). In a mystical sense, the "slave" is the psychic self of man, and the "Son" is his spiritual Self or Logos;

know that you are Abraham's seed; but you
are seeking to kill me, because this saying of
mine does not make progress in you.[1] *I* speak
what I have seen with my Father; therefore,

---

the latter abides in "the Father's house," while the former
has to pass through the cycle of incarnations until it is
freed by becoming one with its Logos. Paulos uses the
same metaphor in *Gal.* iv. 1-7, and adds to it an explanation of the esoteric meaning of the story of Isaac and Ish-
mael (*Gen.* xvi.; xxi.), to show that the man of flesh, the
carnal nature, has no share in the Son's inheritance: " It
is written that Abraham had two sons, one by the slave-
girl, and one by the free woman. But the [son] by the
slave-girl was born according to the flesh, and the [son]
by the free woman [was born] through the promise.
Which [tales of old time] are told with a hidden meaning. For these [women] are two compacts, one [ratified]
from Mount Sinai, which is Hagar giving birth to [her
children] in slavery. For this 'Hagar' *is* Mount Sinai in
Arabia, and corresponds to Hierousalêm [as she is] now,
for *she*, with *her* children, is enslaved. Now, Hierousalêm
[as she is] above, who is our mother, is the free woman.
. . . Now, Brothers, *we*, [who were born] according to
Isaac, are children of the promise. . . . But what says
the writing? ' Banish the slave-girl and her son; for
the son of the slave-girl shall *not* inherit with the son of
the free woman.' And so, Brothers, we are not children
of the slave-girl, but of the free woman. In this freedom the Anointed set us free. Stand firm, therefore,
and do not be caught again in a yoke of slavery " (iv.
22-v. 1).

[1] They had gained a little of the higher knowledge, but
had ceased to advance in it through clinging to their an-
cestral creed.

do *you* what you have heard[1] from your Father!"

They answered and said to him:

"*Our* Father is Abraham."

Iêsous says to them:

"If you were children of Abraham, you would do the works of Abraham; but *now* you are seeking to kill me, a man who has spoken to you the Truth, which I heard from The God. Abraham did not do this [sin]. *You* are doing the works of *your* Father."

They said to him, therefore:

"We have not been born of fornication[2]; we have one Father, The God."

Iêsous said to them:

"If The God were your Father, you would love *me*, for *I* came forth from The God, and am here; for not of myself have I come, but *he* sent me. Why do you not see into this speech of mine? Because you can not listen to *my* saying. *You* are from the Accuser's Father,[3]

---

[1] The Sinaitic reads, "seen"; the Beza, "seen with your Father."

[2] Marriage was used as a symbol of union with the higher nature; and fornication or adultery was used for following false Gods — the Nature-spirits and ghosts of the dead.

[3] Or, "your Father, the Accuser"; or, rather, "the Accuser-Father." The Accuser is a personification of the blind concupiscence of matter, which is the foe of the formative power of the Logos. In man it is the procreative

and the longings[1] of your Father you will to
go on doing. *He* was a man-slayer from a
First-principle, and did not keep his place[2] in
the Truth, because there is no Truth in him.
When he speaks the False,[3] he speaks from his
own; because he is a falsifier, and [so is] *his*[4]
Father. And because *I* say the Truth, you do
not believe me. Which of you reproaches me
about sin? If I say a Truth, why do *you* not
believe me? He who is of The God hears the
words of The God; for this [reason] *you* do not
hear [them], because you are not of The God."

instinct, by which he is "born from below" and held in
the cycle of reincarnations, whereas through the Logos
he is "born from above" and gains freedom. The psychic substance (*gaia*) is saturated with sexuality, and until
a man is purified he can not rise beyond the psychic world
and reach the spiritual planes of being.

[1] Gr. *epithumia*, desire, yearning, lust; the vital impulse,
or longing for sensation. Being unpurified men (*choïkoi*),
they follow the longings of the flesh, and are slaves to
the illusions of matter.

[2] He is the dual-principle or tempting snake in the allegory of the fall into generation; falling from heaven (the
world of Truth), he caused the fall of man. Among the
Gnostics he was represented as the bad serpent (*kakodai-
môn*, evil genius), as opposed to the good serpent (*agatho-
daimôn*, good genius). The one is the Logos; the other,
his Shadow, the kosmic principle of Illusion, which is the
Father of the Accuser. The latter is the sex-principle
after the fall into generation.

[3] Gr. *pseudos*, untruth, falsehood.

[4] That is, the Accuser's — *autou* (his) referring to *diabolou*.

The Ioudaians answered and said to him:

"Say we not well that y o u are a Samareitan, and have a spook ?"[1]

Iêsous answered:

"I have no 'spook'; but I honor my Father, and *you* dishonor me. But *I* do not seek my Radiance; there is one who seeks and judges. Amên, Amên, I say to you, If any one gives heed to this saying of mine, he surely shall not see death throughout the On-going."

The Ioudaians said to him, therefore:

"Now we *know* that y o u have a spook. Abraham died, and the Seers[2]; and *y o u* say, ' If any one gives heed to my saying, he surely shall not see[3] death throughout the On-going.' Surely *y o u* are not a greater [patriarch] than our Father Abraham, who died! The Seers, too, died! Whom do y o u make yourself?"

Iêsous answered:

"If *I* make myself Radiant, my Radiance is

---

[1] Iêsous having explained that all true spiritual inspiration comes from The God, whereas psychic inspiration is illusionary and comes from the Accuser, or animal world-soul (*anima bruta*), his ignorant hearers, upon whom his words are utterly wasted, assert that he is speaking under the inspiration of an obsessing ghost, or *larva*. It will be noticed that such humorous contrasts are frequently introduced in this *Evangel*, in which literalism and unspirituality are unsparingly satirized.

[2] *Zech.* i. 5.

[3] The Sinaitic and the Beza read, "taste."

nothing; it is my Father who makes me Radiant, of whom *you* say that he is your God — and you have not known him. But *I* know him, and if I should say that I do not know him, I shall be the same as you, a falsifier; but I do know him, and I pay heed to his saying. Abraham, your Father, became ecstatic,[1] so that he might see *my* day, and he saw [it] and was glad."

The Ioudaians therefore said to him:

"Y o u are not yet fifty years old, and have y o u seen Abraham?"

Iêsous said to them:

" Amên, Amên, I say to you, Before Abraham came into being *I Am.*"[2]

Then they picked up stones to hurl at him; but Iêsous made himself invisible,[3] and went out of the temple-courts, passing through the midst of them, and thus going unnoticed.

And passing on, he saw a man blind from birth. And his pupils asked him, saying:

[1] See note 1, p. 114.

[2] That is, "Before Abraham came into the sphere of transition (*genesis*) *I am* in the ever-being."

[3] Literally, "was withdrawn from sight." That this was done magically was admitted by the older commentators; but more recent expositors have tortured the Greek in every conceivable way to get rid of the "difficulty," and have rejected the final words of the sentence on wholly insufficient evidence.

"*Rabbi*, who sinned, this [man] or his parents, that he should be born blind?"

Iêsous answered:

"Neither did this [man] 'sin,' nor his parents; but [he is thus afflicted in order] that the works of The God might become manifest in him. [1] *I* must be working the works of him who sent me, [2] while it is day; night is coming, when no one *can* work. While I am in the world, I am the Light of the world."

Having said these [words], he spit on the ground, and made mud out of the spittle, and smeared the mud upon the blind [man's] eyes, and said to him:

[1] While it is true that every evil that befalls a man is due to his own acts in the same or some preceding life, the purpose of the Law is not punishment, but enlightenment. For through suffering and sorrow the soul learns to recognize the Light of the Logos.

[2] The Vatican reads, "*We* must be working . . . of him who sent me," while the Sinaitic has, "who sent us." This curious variation would indicate that there was an older reading which has been purposely changed so as to conceal the fact that Iêsous spoke in the plural, whether as the collective Logos, the host of souls, or, in a personal way, as one of an order of Initiates, doubtless that of the *therapeutai*, or "healers." That the text has been tampered with is evident from a number of passages where the peculiar construction of the Greek shows plainly, in some instances, that two or more variant readings have been unskilfully combined, and, in others, that words have been deleted. In the above passage the work of altering the text was not thoroughly carried out. The "we" occurs also in iii. 11.

"Go and wash[1] [y o u r eyes] in the swimming-bath of Silôam" (which is interpreted "Sent").

He went away, therefore, and washed [his eyes], and came back having sight. The neighbors, therefore, and those who were used to seeing him before, because he was a beggar, said:

"Is not this [man] he who sat and begged?"

Some said, "This is he"; others, "No; but he is like him."

He said:

"*I* am he."

They said to him, therefore:

"How were y o u r eyes opened?"

He answered:

"A man, who is called Iêsous, made [some] mud, and smeared my eyes, and said to me, 'Go to Silôam and wash [them].' And then, having gone away and washed [them], I received sight."

Therefore they said to him:

"Where is that [man]?"

He said:

"I do not know."

They bring to the Pharisaians him who was once blind. Now, it was a Sabbath when

[1] Gr. *niptein*, to wash (as the face or hands); the word is not used for "to bathe." A magical virtue was attributed to saliva, and a lustral or expiatory virtue to water.

Iêsous made the mud, and opened his eyes.
The Pharisaians, also, therefore asked him,
again, *how* he received sight. And he said to
them :

" He put mud on my eyes, and I washed
[them], and I have sight."

Some of the Pharisaians, therefore, said,
" This man is not from The God, because he
does not keep the Sabbath." Others said,
" How can a man who is a wrong-doer do such
signs ? " And there was a division among
them. They say, therefore, to him who was
once blind :

" What, again, do *y o u* say about him, in that
he opened y o u r eyes ? "

And he said :

" He is a Seer."

The Ioudaians, therefore, did not believe
concerning him, that he had been blind and
had received his sight, till they had called the
parents of [the man] himself who had received
sight, and asked them, saying :

" Is this [man] your son, of whom *you* say
that he was born blind ? How is it, then, that
now he has sight ? "

Then his parents answered and said to them :

" We know that this [man] is our son, and
that he was born blind ; but how it is that he
now has sight we do not know, or who opened
his eyes *we* do not know. Ask himself — he

has reached maturity; he will speak about himself."

His parents said these [things] because they were afraid of the Ioudaians; for already the Ioudaians had come to an agreement that if any one should confess him [to be] an Anointed, he should become an outcast from the assembly. For this [reason], his parents said, "He has reached maturity, ask himself." For a second time, therefore, they called the man who had been blind, and said to him:

"Give glory[1] to The God; *we* know that this man is a sinner."

He, therefore, answered and said:

"Whether he is a sinner, I know not. One thing I do know, that having been blind, I now have sight."

They said to him, therefore:

"What did he do to y o u ? *How* did he open y o u r eyes ? "

He answered them:

"I have told you already, and you did not listen. Why do you want to hear [it] again ? Perhaps *you* also want to become his pupils !"

They heaped abuse upon him, and said:

" *Y o u* are a pupil of that [man], but *we* are pupils of Môsês. *We* know that The God has spoken to Môsês; but as for this [man], we do not know whence he is."

[1] See note 2, p. 77.

The man answered and said to them:

"Why, in this [admission] is [something] wonderful — that *you* do not know whence he is! And he opened my eyes, and we *do* know that The God does not hear sinners; but if any one be God-fearing, and does his will, this [man] he hears. Since this On-going it has not been heard that any one opened the eyes of a [man] born blind. If *this* [man] was not [sent] from a God, he could do nothing."

They answered and said to him:

"In sins *y o u* were begotten entirely, and do *y o u* teach *us* ?"

And they hurled him outside. Iêsous heard that they [had] hurled him outside, and having found him, he said to him:

"Do *y o u* believe in the Son of the Man[1]?"

And *he* answered and said:

"Who is he, Master, that I may believe in him?"

Iêsous said to him:

"Y o u have even seen him, and he who is speaking with y o u is *he*."

And he said:

"I believe [it], Master"; and he made obeisance[2] to him.

---

[1] Although some manuscripts read, "Son of The God," the weight of authority lies with the reading, "Son of the Man."

[2] That is, prostrated himself, making the *salâm*.

And Iêsous said:

"For a distinction [1] *I* came into this world, that those who do not see may have sight, and those who see may become blind." [2]

Those of the Pharisaians who were with him heard these [words], and said to him:

"Surely *we* are not blind?"

Iêsous said to them:

"If you were blind, you would not have sin; but now you say, 'We have sight,' your sin, therefore, abides. [3] Amên, Amên, I say to you, He who does not go in through the door into the sheep-fold, but climbs up from another quarter, *he* is a thief and a bandit [4]; but he who does go in through the door is a shepherd of the sheep. To this [shepherd] the door-keeper opens, and the sheep hear his voice, and he calls his own sheep according to name, and leads them out. And when he has driven out

---

[1] Gr. *krima*, a decision, decree; a matter for consideration. The word is not found elsewhere in this *Evangel*.

[2] The common people were gaining spiritual insight, while their priestly rulers were becoming spiritually blind.

[3] The many, the useless portion of mankind, are irresponsible because of their blindness and ignorance; they can hardly be said to have risen above the animal kingdom, or to be accountable for their actions. But once a man has seen the spiritual Light he becomes responsible for all his words and deeds. "When one knows [what is] right, and does not do [it], to him it is sin" (*Jas.* iv. 17).

[4] Gr. *lêstês*, a plunderer, pirate, brigand.

all his own sheep, he goes in front of them, and the sheep go with him, because they know his voice; but with a strange [man] they will not go, but will run away from him, because they do not know the voice of those who are strangers."

This commonplace[1] Iêsous said to them; but *they* did not know what the [things] were which he spoke to them. Again, therefore, Iêsous said to them:

"Amên, Amên, I say to you, *I* am the door of the sheep. All who came before *me* are thieves and bandits; but the sheep did not hear them.[2] *I* am the door; through *me* if any one enters in, he shall be kept safe, and shall go in, and go out and find pasture. The thief does not come except that he may steal, and kill, and

[1] Gr. *paroimia*, a wayside saying, saw, proverb; an ancient maxim having an esoteric meaning.

[2] That is, would not recognize them when called. The mystic "door of Iêsous" is the opening of the "third eye," or eye of the Seer; and the psychic visions and other vague, distorted glimpses of truth which precede the full spiritual illumination are the "thieves and bandits." The Gnostics and Manichæans, who knew perfectly well the inner meaning, taunted the orthodox by pointing out that this passage repudiated the Ioudaian Seers who came before Iêsous. The words "before me" were accordingly expunged from many manuscripts, and a puerile explanation was given by Augustine and others that only false Seers *came*, true Seers being *sent*. In the *Book of Enoch* the allegory of the Good Shepherd is given in a more complete form.

destroy. *I* came that they may have Life, and may have [it] above measure. *I* am that Good Shepherd.[1] That Good Shepherd gives up his ghost[2] for the sheep. But he who is a hireling, and is not a shepherd, whose own the sheep are not, sees the wolf coming, and leaves the sheep and runs away, and the wolf snatches them out, and scatters the sheep. Now, he who is a hireling runs away, because he *is* a hireling, and does not care about the sheep. *I* am that Good Shepherd; and I know mine, and am known of mine, even as the Father knows me, and *I* know the Father; and I give up my ghost for the sheep. Other sheep also I have, which are not of this fold; those also must I bring, and they will hear my voice; and there

[1] Hermês, the pastoral God, who shepherded the starry flocks, and was the Interpreter of the Gods, was mystically what Iêsous here represents himself to be. He was called the " Saviour " (*sôtêr*) and the " Oracle " (*logios*).

[2] Gr. *psuchê*, the psychic or *vital* body. It is neither the " life " nor the " soul," but is an ethereal counterpart of the physical body and the vehicle of the life-principle. It may leave the physical body during the sleep of the latter, and appear at a distance as a wraith or phantom. After death it becomes the " ghost," or " shade," in the psychic world (*hadês*). The expression " give up his *shade* " was equivalent to the modern " give up his life." The word " ghost " is an unsatisfactory rendering, but in English there is no word of identical meaning with the Greek term; yet in the older Greek *psuchê* is strictly the wraith of a departed person.

shall become one flock, one shepherd. For this [reason] the Father loves me, because *I* give up my ghost that I may take it back.[1] No one takes it away from me, but *I* give it up of myself. I have authority to give it up, and I have authority to take it back. This command I received from my Father."

A division again arose among the Ioudaians because of these sayings; and many of them said:

"He has a spook, and is raving; why are you listening to him?" Others said: "These words are not those of one spook-possessed. Can a spook open the eyes of the blind?"

Now, there took place [the festival] "Initiation"[2] at Hierousalêm. It was winter. And Iêsous was walking in the temple-courts, in Solomôn's portico. The Ioudaians, therefore, surrounded him, and said to him:

---

[1] Here there is a play on the word *psuchê*. While "giving up the ghost" has the colloquial allusion to death, it here means abandoning the psychic body for the spiritual body (*sôma pneumatikon*). See Appendix II., "The Birth from Above."

[2] Gr. *enkainia*, renewal, renovation, consecration. This festival of eight days was said to be in commemoration of the purification of the temple at Hierousalêm after it had been profaned. It was also called "Lights" (*phôta*) (Jos., *Ant.*, xii. 7).

"How long will y o u hold us in suspense [1]?
If *y o u* are the Anointed, tell us openly."

Iêsous answered them:

"I have told you, and you do not believe
[me]. The works which *I* do in the Name of
my Father, these works bear witness about me.
But *you* do not have faith, for you are not of
my sheep. *My* sheep hear my voice, and *I*
know them, and they go with me, and *I* give
them On-going Life, and they shall not at all
die throughout the On-going, and no one shall
snatch them out of my hand. My Father, who
has given [them] to me, is a greater [God] than
all, [2] and no one can snatch [anything] out of
the Father's hand. *I* and the Father are one."

Again, therefore, the Ioudaians were holding
in their hands stones, that they might stone
him. Iêsous answered them:

"Many good works did I show you from my
Father; for which work of them do you stone
me ? "

The Ioudaians answered him, saying:

"We do not stone y o u on account of a *good*
work, but on account of railing, and because
y o u, who are a man, make yourself a God."

Iêsous answered them:

[1] Literally, "exalt our ghost," *psuchê* being the seat of
the sensations — doubt, fear, and the like.

[2] The Vatican reads, "What my Father has given me is
a greater [gift] than all."

"Is it not written in your Law, '*I* said, You are Gods'[1]? If he called *them* Gods to whom the Thought of The God came — and the writing can not be done away with — do *you* say of him whom the Father purified and sent into the world, 'Y o u rail,' because I said, 'I am a *Son* of The God'? If I do not do the works of my Father, do not believe me; but if I do, even if you do not believe *me*, believe the works, so that you may see into, and *know*, [2] that the Father [is] in *me*, and *I* [am] in the Father."[3]

Again, therefore, they sought to take him, and again he got away out of their hand.[4] And he went back again to the other side of the Iordanos, to the place where Iôannês was at first lustrating; and there he abode. And many came to him, and they said:

"Iôannês, indeed, did no sign; but all [things] that Iôannês said about this [man] were true."

And many believed in him there.

Now, there was a certain one lying sick, Lazaros, of Bêthania, from the village of Mariam and Martha, her sister. And it was the [same] Mariam who anointed the Master with

[1] *Ps.* lxxxii. 6.

[2] The Sinaitic reads, "that you may know and believe."

[3] Or, "that as the Father [is] in *me*, so *I* [am] in the Father."

[4] See note 3, p. 129.

scented oil, [1] and wiped his feet with her hair, whose brother Lazaros was sick. The sisters, therefore, sent to him, saying:

"Master, see, he whom y o u dearly love is sick."

But when Iêsous heard [it], he said:

"This sickness is not to death, but for the Radiance of The God, that the Son of The God may be made Radiant through it."

Now, Iêsous loved [2] Martha, and her sister, and Lazaros. When, therefore, he heard that he was sick, at the time indeed he abode two days in the place where he was; then after this [stay] he says to the pupils:

"Let us go into Ioudaia again."

The pupils say to him:

"*Rabbi*, just now the Ioudaians were seeking to stone y o u; and are y o u going back there?"

Iêsous answered:

"Are there not twelve hours in the day? If one walks in the day, he does not stumble, because he sees the light of *this* world; but if one walks in the night, he stumbles, because the Light is not in him."

These [words] he said; and after this [speech] he says to them:

"Lazaros, our friend, has fallen asleep; but I

[1] Gr. *muron*, any oil, as olive-oil, scented with perfumes.

[2] The Beza has, "dearly loved" (*philein*).

am going that I may wake him out of his sleep."

The pupils, therefore, said to him:

"Master, if he has fallen asleep, he will be saved." [1]

Now, Iêsous had said [it] about his death; but *they* thought that he said [it] of the repose of sleep. Then, therefore, Iêsous said to them openly:

"Lazaros is dead. [2] And for your sake I am glad that I was not there, so that you may have faith. But let us go to him."

Thômas, therefore— he who is called "Twin" [3] — said to his fellow-pupils:

"Let *us* go also, that we may die with him." [4]

Iêsous, therefore, having come, found that by this time he had been four days in the tomb. Now, Bêthania was near Hierousalêm, about fifteen furlongs distant. And many of the Ioudaians had come to the [women] who were about Martha and Mariam that they might console them about their brother. Martha, therefore, when she heard that Iêsous was coming, went to meet him; but Mariam still sat in the house. Martha, therefore, said to Iêsous:

---

[1] Gr. *sôzesthai*, to be saved, healed; to get well. See note 3, p. 106.

[2] Literally, "Lazaros died."

[3] Gr. *didumos*, twofold, double; a twin (brother).

[4] That is, with Iêsous, who was threatened with stoning.

"Master, if y o u had been here, my brother would not be dead. And now, even, I know that whatever [things] y o u will ask of The God, The God will give y o u."

Iêsous says to her:

"Y o u r brother shall awaken." [1]

Martha says to him:

"I know that he will awaken — at the 'Awakening' on the last day!"

Iêsous said to her:

"*I* am the Awakening and the Life. He who believes in *me*, even if he die, [2] shall live; and every one who is alive and believes in *me* shall not die throughout the On-going. [3] Do y o u believe this [teaching]?"

[1] Gr. *anastênai*, to stand up; rise from sleep, wake up. This word is nearly synonymous with *egerthênai;* but properly the latter means "to rise (from sleep)," while *anastênai* signifies "to rise (for action)," and this distinction is generally observed in the Synoptics. But the writer of the fourth *Evangel* seems to have transposed the two words, giving to *anastênai* the shade of meaning "to awake," probably in order to use *anastasis* poetically as "awakening" instead of "rising-up," or "resurrection," in which latter sense it is employed by the Synoptic writers.

[2] Or, "if he be dead."

[3] One who attains to the purely spiritual consciousness is not under the sway of death even while incarnated in the mortal body; and when "born from above" in the sidereal body (*sôma pneumatikon*) his life is continuous, without loss of memory between incarnations, throughout the world-cycle.

She says to him:

"Yes, Master; *I* have believed that *y o u* are the Anointed, the Son of The God, who is coming into the world."

And having said these [words], she went away and called Mariam, her sister, secretly saying:

"The Teacher is arrived, and calls y o u."

She, when she heard [it], rises up quickly and comes to him. Now, Iêsous had not yet come into the village, but was [still] in the place where Martha met him. The Ioudaians, therefore, who were with her in the house, and were consoling her, when they saw Mariam rise quickly and go out, followed her, saying:

"She is going to the tomb, to wail[1] there."

Mariam, therefore, when she came where Iêsous was, on seeing him fell at his feet, saying:

"Master, if y o u had been here, my brother would not have died."

Iêsous, therefore, when he saw her wailing, and the Ioudaians wailing who came out with her, became imperious[2] in the Breath and stirred himself up, and said:

---

[1] To pay the tribute of loud lamentation for the dead.

[2] Gr. *embrimasthai*, to be furious; to roar; to issue orders under a threat. Here it denotes the arousing of the Breath by the imperious magnetic will, thus stirring up the forces preparatory to a feat of magic — the raising of Lazaros.

"Where have you laid him?"

They say to him:

"Master, come and see."

Iêsous shed tears. The Ioudaians, therefore, said, "See, how dearly he loved him!" But some of them said, "Could not this [healer], who opened the eyes of one who was blind, have caused that this [friend] should not die?" Iêsous, therefore, again becoming imperious [1] in himself, comes to the tomb. Now, it was a cave, and a stone lay upon it. Iêsous says:

"Take away the stone."

Martha, the sister of the dead [man], says to him:

"Master, by this time he smells, for it is the fourth day." [2]

Iêsous says to her:

"Have I not told y o u that if y o u will have faith, y o u shall see the Radiance of The God?"

They took away the stone, therefore; and Iêsous lifted up his eyes above, [3] and said:

[1] The thaumaturgic frenzy previously aroused having subsided through his sorrow for the dead.

[2] This is given merely as a surmise of Martha. It was the popular belief that until the expiration of the third day after death the *psuché* of the deceased was still united to the physical body, into which it could be recalled by the will-power of the magician. Hence the Greeks resorted to special rites (*protrita*) during that period. To sever the ghost from the dead body, cremation was resorted to.

[3] That is, using the inner or spiritual senses.

"Father, I return thanks to you because you heard me. (Now, *I* knew that every time you hear me; but for the people's sake who are standing around I said [it], that they may believe that *you* sent me.)"

And having said these [words], he cried with a mighty voice:

"Lazaros! Hither, outside!"[1]

Forth came the dead [man], bound feet and hands with bandages, and his face was bound round with a handkerchief. Iêsous says to them:

"Untie him, and permit [him] to withdraw."

Many of the Ioudaians, therefore—those who had come to Mariam and had seen the things he had done—believed in him. But some of them went away to the Pharisaians, and told them the things Iêsous had done. Therefore the archpriests and the Pharisaians assembled a council, and they said:

"What are we to do? For this man does many signs. If we let him alone in this way, all [the people] will believe in him; and the Romans will come, and take away both our place and our [priestly] class."[2]

---

[1] Addressing the ghost, who is outside the physical body, and ordering it to return by the call, "Hither," "Come here" (*deuro*).

[2] Gr. *ethnos*, a number of people living together; a band of men, tribe, family, race; a particular class or caste. It

But a certain one of them, Kaiaphas, being Archpriest of that year, said to them:

"*You* know nothing. Nor do you take into account that it is to our own interest that one man should die because of the common people, and not the whole class perish."

Now, he said this [prediction] not from himself, but being Archpriest of that year, he declared as a Seer[1] that Iêsous was about to die for the class, and not for the class alone, but that he might also gather together into one the children of The God who were scattered abroad. From that day, therefore, they consulted together that they might kill him. Iêsous, therefore, no longer walked openly among the Ioudaians, but went away from that place into the region near the desert, to a city called

was because the growing influence of Iêsous among the common people was lessening the authority of the sacerdotal caste that the latter conspired to have him put to death. His efforts were wholly to restore the esoteric system, doing away with exoteric ritualistic observances and freeing the people from the tyranny of their degenerate priestly rulers. That the Ioudaian *nation* was in no danger of extinction as such is shown by the fact that Pilatos voluntarily offered to make Iêsous their ruler — which would have resulted in the downfall of the sacerdotal class. But the crucifixion of Iêsous is a purely mystical allegory of the birth "from above," and has no historical basis.

[1] Gr. *prophêteuein*, to declare in the name of a God, to state as a Seer.

Ephraim, and there he passed the time with his pupils.

Now, the "Passing-over" of the Ioudaians was near; and many went up to Hierousalêm out of that region, before the "Passing-over," that they might purify themselves. They sought, therefore, for Iêsous, and said to one another, as they stood in the temple-courts: "What do *you* think? That he will not come to the festival?"

Now, the archpriests and the Pharisaians had given a command that, if any one knew where he was, he should lay information, so that they might take him.

Iêsous, therefore, six days before the "Passing-over," came to Bêthania, where Lazaros was, whom Iêsous raised from among the dead ones. They made him, therefore, a dinner there, and Martha waited on [him]; but Lazaros was one of those reclining [at table] with him. Mariam, therefore, taking a pound of scented oil, of real nard, very costly, anointed the feet of Iêsous, and wiped his feet with her hair; and the house was filled with the odor of the scented oil. One of his pupils, therefore, Ioudas, [the son] of Simôn Iskariôtês — he who was about to deliver him up — says:

"Why was not this scented oil sold for three hundred denarii,[1] and given to the beggars?"

[1] About fifty dollars.

Now, he said this [complaint], not because he
cared about the beggars, but because he was a
thief, and he held the money-box,[1] and had the
carrying of the things thrown [into it].

Iêsous, therefore, said:

"Let her alone. She has kept it until the
day of my preparation for the tomb.[2] For you
have the beggars with yourselves all the time,
but *me* you do not have all the time."

A great crowd, therefore, of the Ioudaians
knew that he was there; and they came, not on
account of Iêsous only, but that they might see
Lazaros also, whom he raised from among the
dead ones. Now, the archpriests consulted
together, that they might kill Lazaros also, because on account of him many of the Ioudaians
were going away and believing in Iêsous.

On the morrow the crowd[3] who had come to
the festival, having heard that Iêsous was coming to Hierousalêm, took the leaf-stems of the
palm-trees, and went out for the purpose of
meeting him, and cried out:

[1] Gr. *glôssokomon*, a box for holding valuables. Originally the word was applied to the box in which pipers
carried their wind-instruments (*glôssidas*).

[2] Gr. *entaphiasmos*, embalming or otherwise preparing
the corpse for the tomb. The statement of Iêsous is a
prediction of his "crucifixion" in the near future. The
Vatican reads, "Suffer her to keep it," etc.

[3] Here, as in the preceding paragraph, some manuscripts
read, "a great crowd."

"*Hosanna*[1]*!* Praised [is] he who comes in the Name of the Master! The Ruler of Israêl!"[2]

And Iêsous, having found a little ass,[3] seated himself upon it, as it is written:

"Fear not, Daughter of Siôn! Behold, your Ruler comes, seated upon an ass's colt!"[4]

Now, his pupils did not see into these [things] at first; but when Iêsous was made Radiant, then they called to mind that these [things] had been written about him and they had done these [things] to him.

The people who were with him, therefore, bore witness that he called Lazaros out of the tomb, and raised him from among the dead ones. For this [reason], also, the people went out to meet him, because they heard that he had done this sign. The Pharisaians, therefore, said to themselves:

"You see that you are of no use at all! See, the world is going away after him!"

Now, there were certain Hellênes among those who were going up to worship at the

---

[1] Meaning "Save now!"

[2] *Ps.* cxviii. 25, 26; *Zeph.* iii. 15.

[3] The black cross on the shoulders of the ass probably gave the animal its place in symbolism. The account of the triumphal entry into Hierousalêm is given in all four of the *Evangels*, but Matthew speaks of a she-ass and her colt.

[4] *Zech.* ix. 9.

festival. These [men], therefore, came to Philippos — who was from Bêthsaida of Galilaia — and asked him, saying:

"Master, we wish to see Iêsous."

Philippos goes and tells Andreas. And, again, Andreas and Philippos come, and they tell Iêsous. And Iêsous answers them, saying:

"The hour has come, that the Son of the Man should be made Radiant. Amên, Amên, I say to you, Unless the grain[1] of the wheat falls to the earth and dies, it abides by itself, alone; but if it dies, it bears much fruit. He who loves his ghost causes it to perish,[2] and he who hates his ghost in *this* world shall keep it throughout On-going Life.[3] If any one serve *me*, let him follow *me*, and where *I* am, there also shall be this server of mine; if any one serve *me*, the Father will honor him. Now my ghost is stirred up,[4] and what shall I say? 'Father, save me from this hour'? But it was for this [end] that I came into this hour! 'Father, make y o u r Name Radiant'?"

[1] Gr. *kokkos*, a kernel.

[2] The Beza has, "will lose it."

[3] The perfect man, or Initiate, preserves the same psychic body from incarnation to incarnation; whereas the unpurified man loses the psychic body, which dies in the psychic world after the dissolution of the physical body.

[4] Referring to the psychic exaltation that precedes the pneumatic birth "from above," which birth is allegorized in the crucifixion.

There came, therefore, a Voice out of the Sky:

"I have both made [it] Radiant, and I will make [it] Radiant again."

The people, therefore, who stood and heard [it] said that there had been thunder. Others said, "A Messenger has spoken to him." Iêsous answered and said:

"Not on account of *me* has this Voice come, but on account of *you*. Now there is a separating of this world. Now is the Leader of this world [1] about to be cast outside. And *I*, if I be lifted up on high from the Earth, will draw all [men] [2] to myself."

Now, he said this [similitude], showing by a sign what kind of death he was about to die. The people, therefore, answered him:

"*We* heard out of the Law that the Anointed abides throughout the On-going; and how is it that *y o u* say that the Son of the Man must be lifted up on high? Who *is* this 'Son of the Man'?"

---

[1] That is, all material taint is to be removed by the purifying action of the Breath in the mystic crucifixion. The "Leader (*archôn*) of this world" is the Accuser (*diabolos*). See note 1, p. 125.

[2] The Sinaitic and Beza read, "all [things]." Every man who becomes self-purified raises the level of the entire human race, through the psychical and spiritual ties which unite all men; and in this sense every Initiate is a Saviour.

Iêsous, therefore, said to them:

"For a little time yet the Light is in you. Walk while you have the Light, so that Darkness may not overtake[1] you; and he who walks in the Darkness does not know where he is going. While you have the Light, believe in the Light, so that you may become Sons of Light."

These [things] Iêsous spoke, and going away he became concealed from them. But though he had done so many signs in front of them, they did not believe in him, so that the saying of Hêsaias the Seer might be fulfilled, which he said:

"Master, who has believed that which we heard,
And to whom was the arm of the Master uncovered?"[2]

For this [reason] they were not able to believe, because again Hêsaias said:

"He has blinded their eyes,
And petrified[3] their heart,

---

[1] See note 1, p. 74.

[2] *Isa.* liii. 1.

[3] Gr. *pôroun*, to turn into stone, petrify. The allusion is to the "philosopher's stone," the petrified "third eye," which is the "heart" of the brain, and the organ of noëtic action. "A stone which the Builders [mankind before the

> So that they might not see with their eyes,
> And discern [1] with their heart,
> And turn themselves about, [2] and I should
> heal them." [3]

Hêsaias said these [words] because he saw
his Radiance, and spoke about him.   Still,
however, even of the leaders many believed
in him; but on account of the Pharisaians
they did not admit [it], that they might not
become outcasts from the assembly.   For they
loved the Radiance of the Men rather than the
Radiance of The God. [4]   But Iêsous cried out
and said :

fall into generation] rejected, the same is become the apex
of the angle [with the two eyes it forms a triangle] ; this
came into being from the Master, and it is wondrous in our
eyes " (*Matt.* xxi. 42 ; also *Mk.* xii. 10, 11, and *Lk.* xx. 17).

[1] Gr. *noein*, to perceive by the mind, know intuitively,
cognize.

[2] That is, looking *within*, instead of *without;* all true
knowledge being interior and noëtic, and the empirical
knowledge gained through the outer senses being illusionary.

[3] *Isa.* vi. 10.

[4] They recognized Iêsous as the Teacher of the new
cycle, but had not the moral courage to endure ostracism
throughout his cycle for the sake of the Eternal.   For
during the cycle of Iêsous (2,155 years of the Sun in
Pisces) the Mysteries have been unknown in the outer
world, and the followers of the esoteric Truth have been
persecuted by the exoteric church, by whom in the early
centuries they were excommunicated as " heretics."

"He who believes in *me* believes, not in *me*, but in him who sent me; and he who sees *me* sees him who sent me. *I*, a Light,[1] have come into the world, that every one who believes in *me* may not abide in the Darkness. And if any one hears my words, and does not believe [them],[2] *I* do not separate him; for I did not come that I might separate the world, but that I might save the world. He who sets *me* aside, and does not accept my words, has that which separates him — the saying which I spoke, *that* will separate him in the last day. Because *I* did not speak from myself; but the Father who sent me, *he* gave me a command, what I should say, and what I should speak; and I know that his command is On-going Life. The [words], therefore, which *I* speak, as the Father has said [them] to me, so do I speak."

Now, before the festival of the "Passing-over," Iêsous, knowing that his hour had come, so that he should pass on out of this world to

---

[1] Compare *Jas.* i. 17: "Every good bequest and every perfect gift is from above, coming down from the Father of the Lights, with whom there can be no alternation, or shadow of turning " — referring to the alternating seasons, and the shadow on the sun-dial, and thus contrasting the Eternal Father of Lights with manifested Time as measured by the heavenly bodies in Space.

[2] The received text, following the Vatican, reads, " does not keep [them]."

the Father, having loved his own who were in
the world, loved them throughout the perfecting-period.[1] And as dinner was going on —
the Accuser having by this time put [it] into
the heart of Ioudas, [the son] of Simôn Iskariôtês, that he should deliver him up — Iêsous,
knowing that the Father had given all [things]
into his hands, and that he came forth from a
God, and was going to The God, rises from the
dinner, and lays aside his outer garments, and
taking a towel, girded himself. Then he puts
water into the wash-bowl, and began to wash
the feet of the pupils and to wipe [them] with
the towel with which he was girded. He comes,
therefore, to Simôn Petros; and *he* says to
him:

"Master, do *y o u* wash my feet?"

Iêsous answered and said to him:

"What *I* am doing *y o u* do not understand
now; but after these [things] y o u will know."

Petros says to him:

"Never throughout the On-going shall y o u
wash *my* feet!"

Iêsous answered him:

"If I do not [thus] wash[2] y o u, y o u have
no part with me."

Simôn Petros says to him:

[1] Gr. *telos*, an end accomplished; being complete or perfect; the period of initiation into the Mysteries.

[2] See note 1, p. 145.

"Master, not my feet only, but also my hands and my head!"

Iêsous says to him:

"He who is fresh-bathed[1] has no need save to wash his feet, but is clean all over. *You*, also, are clean, but not all."

For he knew the one who was to deliver him up; for this [reason] he said, "Not all of you are clean."

When, therefore, he had washed their feet, and taken up his outer garments, and reclined [at table] again, he said to them:

"Do you discern what I have done to you? *You* call me 'The Teacher' and 'The Master,' and you say well; for [so] I am. If, therefore, *I*, the Master and the Teacher, washed *your* feet, *you* also are under a debt to wash each other's feet; for I gave you an example, that as *I* did to you, *you* should do also. Amên, Amên, I say to you, A slave is not greater than his master, nor an emissary greater than he who sent him. If you know these [things], immortal[2] are you if you do them. I do not say [it] about

---

[1] Gr. *louein*, to bathe, to wash (the whole body); as opposed to *niptein*, to wash (the face, hands, etc.).

[2] Gr. *makarios*, for ever blessed. In older Greek the epithet is applied to the Gods as descriptive of their eternal bliss, and has the force of "immortal" rather than simply "blessed" or "happy." Man's yearning for happiness, desire for knowledge, and longing for life reflect the eternal Bliss, Consciousness, and Being of his real Self.

all of you; *I* know whom I chose; but [it had to be] so that the writing may be fulfilled:

> " 'He who eats the bread with me
> Has lifted up his heel against me.' [1]

I tell you even now, before it has come to pass, so that, when it does come to pass, you may believe that *I Am*. Amên, Amên, I say to you, He who receives any one whom I shall send receives *me*, and he who receives *me* receives him who sent me."

Having said these [words], Iêsous was stirred up in the Breath,[2] and bore witness, and said:

"Amên, Amên, I say to you, One of *you* is about to deliver me up."

The pupils, therefore, looked one at another, being in doubt about whom he said [it]. Now, one of his pupils was reclining in the bosom of Iêsous — the one whom Iêsous loved. To this [pupil], therefore, Simôn Petros nods, and says to him:

"Say who it is about whom he said [it]." [3]

And *he*, leaning back on the breast of Iêsous, says to him:

[1] *Ps.* xli. 9. Apparently the metaphor is borrowed from wrestling, denoting treachery by tripping up with the heel.

[2] That is, went into the mantic state, the prophetic frenzy.

[3] The Sinaitic and Beza read, "nods to him that he should inquire who it was of whom he said it."

"Master, who is it?"

Iêsous, therefore, answers:

"It is *he* for whom I shall dip a small mouthful[1] and give it to him."

Then, having dipped the small mouthful, he took and gave it to Ioudas, [the son] of Simôn Iskariôtês. And after the small mouthful, then the Adversary[2] entered into him. Iêsous, therefore, says to him:

"That which *you* do, do quickly."

Now, none of those reclining knew *why* he said this [command] to him; for some thought —seeing that Ioudas held the money-box—that Iêsous says to him, "Buy what we have need of for the festival"; or, that he should give something to the beggars. *He*, therefore, having received the small mouthful, went out directly. Now, it was night. When, therefore, he went out, Iêsous says:

"*Now* the Son of the Man is made Radiant, and The God is made Radiant in him. If The God is made Radiant in him, The God also will make him Radiant in himself, and will directly make him Radiant. Little children, yet a little while I am with you. You will seek me, and as I said to the Ioudaians, 'Where *I* am going, *you* can not come,' I now say to you also. A

---

[1] Gr. *psômion*, a morsel, scrap, sippet.

[2] Gr. *satanas*, adversary; a word derived from the Hebrew.

new command [1] I give you, that you love one
another—that, as I have loved you, so should
you also love one another. By this [token]
shall all [men] know that you are my pupils,
if you have love one for the other."

Simôn Petros says to him:

"Master, *where* are y o u going ?"

Iêsous answered him:

"Where I am going, y o u can not now follow
me; but y o u shall follow me afterwards."

Petros says to him:

"Master, *why* can I not follow y o u *now ?*   I
will give up my ghost for y o u."

Iêsous answers:

"Will y o u give up y o u r ghost for me?
Amên, Amên, I say to y o u, A cock shall not
crow at all, until y o u have utterly denied me
thrice. Let not your heart be stirred up.
Believe in The God, and believe in *me*.[2] In
the house of my Father there are many abid-
ings [3]; but if not so, I would have told you

[1] It is not clear why this should be called a *new* command,
for the same injunction is given in the Mosaic books, as in
Lev. xix. 17, 18.   In *Matt.* v. 43, 44, however, the pupils
are commanded to love their enemies, which precept is not
in the Mosaic Law.

[2] Or, "You believe in The God; believe also in *me*."   Or,
again, according to the Greek idiom, "As you believe in The
God, so believe in *me*."

[3] Gr. *monê*, a staying, tarrying, abiding. Between incarnations the soul rests for a while in the spiritual world,

that I am going to make ready a place for you;
and if I do go and make ready a place for you,
I am coming back, and I will take you to myself, so that where *I* am, *you* also may be. And
where *I* am going, you know; and the Path [1]
you know."

Thômas says to him:

"Master, we do *not* know where y o u are
going; and how can we know the 'path'?"

Iêsous says to him:

"*I* am the Path, and the Truth, and the Life;
no one comes to the Father except through *me*.
If you had known me, you would have known
my Father also; and from now on you do know
him, and have seen him."

Philippos says to him:

"Master, point out the Father to us, and we
are satisfied." [2]

Iêsous says to him:

"Have I been so long a time with you, and

the mystic "house of the Father," the Plêrôma; and when
it has overcome the flesh, having accomplished its purification and won its freedom, it remains permanently in that
spiritual world, and does not incarnate again unless
voluntarily. Hence it is said in the *Apokalypse* (iii. 12):
"The conqueror, I will make him a pillar in the temple of
my God, and he shall not at all go outward any more."

[1] The "path" is the intuitive intellect, which connects
man with his inner God. Its first manifestations are Faith
and Conscience. See note 2, p. 81.

[2] Literally, "it is enough for us."

[yet] y o u do not know me, Philippos? He who
has seen *me* has seen the Father. How is it that
y o u say, 'Point out the Father to us'? Do
y o u not believe that *I* [am] in the Father, and
the Father is in *me?* The words which *I* speak
to you I do not speak from myself; the Father,
who abides in *me*, [speaks them:] he himself
does the works. Believe me [when I say to
you] that *I* [am] in the Father, and the Father
in *me;* but if not so, for the very works' sake
believe me. Amên, Amên, I say to you, He who
believes in *me*, the works which *I* do, *he* also
shall do. Aye, he shall do greater [works] than
these, because *I* am going to my Father, and
whatever you may ask in my Name, that I will
do, so that the Father may be made Radiant in
the Son. If you shall ask anything in my
Name, this [work] I will do. If you love me,
you will give heed to *my* commands; and *I* will
ask the Father, and he will give you another
Advocate,[1] that there may abide with you

---

[1] Gr. *paraklêtos*, a legal assistant, advocate; a helper. The
Advocate is the Breath manifesting in man as a positive
force or creative principle. It is the pure Fire, the *vital*
electricity which awakens the "third eye" of the Seer. The
Accuser (*diabolos*) is the reverse aspect of the same principle;
the two are the forces respectively of generation and
regeneration, of birth "from below" and birth "from
above." The Paraklêtos can manifest only in the purified
ascetic, in whom it becomes the Initiator, the Advocate with
the Father.

throughout the On-going that Breath of the Truth which the world can not receive because it sees it not nor knows it. *You* know it because it abides with you and *is* in you. I will not leave you as orphans; I am coming to you. Yet a little while, and the world sees me no longer; but *you* see me, because *I* am living and *you* are about to be living. In that day *you* shall know that *I* [am] in the Father, and *you* in *me*, and *I* in *you*. He who has my commands, and pays heed to them, *he* it is who loves me; and he who loves me will be loved by my Father, and *I* shall love him, and shall manifest myself to him."

Ioudas—not [the one called] Iskariôtês — says to him:

" Master, what has come about, that you are about to manifest yourself to *us*, and not to the world?"

Iêsous answered and said to him:

" If any one loves me, he will pay heed to my saying; and my Father will love him, and we shall come to him, and make an abiding with him. He who does not love me does not pay heed to my sayings; and the saying which you

---

[1] As Ioudas Iskariôtês corresponds to the Accuser (see note 1, p. 125), the allegory requires this other Ioudas as corresponding to the Advocate. Hence he is shown here as the one who questions Iêsous on this subject, and elicits the teaching concerning the Advocate.

hear is not mine, but the Father's who sent me. These [words] I have spoken to you while abiding with you; but the Advocate, that pure Breath which the Father will send in my Name, *he* will teach you all [Mysteries], and will put you in mind of all [things] which I said to you. Peace *I* forsake[1] for you; *my* peace I give to you; not as the world gives do *I* give to you. Let not your heart be stirred up, neither let it be cowardly.[2] You heard that *I* said to you, 'I am going away, and am coming back to you.' If you loved me, you would have rejoiced that I am going to the Father, because the Father is greater than I. And I have told you now before it happens, so that when it does happen you may believe [me]. I shall not any more speak many [things] with you; for the Leader of the world is coming. And he has nothing in *me*[3]; but—so that the world may know that

[1] Gr. *aphienai*, to cast away, give up, let go. The translation "Peace I *leave* with you" is from the *Vulgate*, which reads *relinquo*, while the Beza has, *pacem dismitto vobis*.

[2] Though Iêsous has given up his peace, and is about to pass through the fiery ordeal of the crucifixion, his pupils, who are still in the psychic stage, could not safely arouse the higher forces.

[3] The Greek of the Beza gives, "and he has nothing to find in *me*," and the Latin, *et in me non habet nihil invenire*. The *Vulgate* has, *et in me non habet quicquam*. Going to his final trial—the crucifixion—Iêsous declares himself prepared for it, being free from all earthly taint.

I love the Father, and as the Father commanded me, so I do—arise, let us go hence.[1]

"*I* am the true Vine, and my Father is the tiller of the soil.[2] Every branch in *me* that does not bear fruit, he takes it away; and every one that does bear fruit, he cleanses,[3] so that it may bear more fruit. Already *you* are clean through the saying which I have spoken to you. Abide in me, and *I* in you.[4] Even as the branch can not bear fruit of itself, unless it abides in the vine, so neither [can] *you*, unless you abide in *me*. *I* am the vine, *you* [are] the branches. He who abides in me, and *I* in him, this [branch] bears much fruit; because apart from me you can do nothing. If any one does not abide in me, he is cast outside, as the branch, and becomes dried-up; and they gather them together,[5] and throw [them] into the fire, and they are burned up. If you abide in me, and my words abide in you, ask whatsoever you

[1] To show that his is a voluntary sacrifice, Iêsous goes forth to meet the Accuser—Ioudas—continuing his discourse as they go out into the night, the simile of the vine being probably suggested by a vine on a trellis at the outer door.

[2] Gr. *geôrgos* ("earth-worker"), a tiller of the soil, laborer, husbandman.

[3] That is, "clears," or "prunes."

[4] Or, more accurately in the English idiom, "Abide in me as *I* [abide] in you."

[5] That is, the withered vine-clippings. The Sinaitic and the Beza read, "they gather it up."

will, and it shall come to pass[1] for you. In this [time] is my Father made Radiant, that you may bear much fruit, and become my pupils.[2] As the Father loved *me*, *I* also loved *you*. Abide in this love of mine. If you shall have paid heed to my commands, you *will* abide in my love, as *I* have paid heed to my Father's commands, and abide in *his* love. These [things] I have spoken to you that *my* joy may abide in you, and *your* joy may be made full. This is my command, that you love one another as I loved you. Greater love than this not any one has—that one should give up his ghost in behalf of his friends. *You* ARE my friends, if you keep doing what [things] *I* command you. I no longer call you slaves, because the slave does not know what his Master is doing; but *you* I have called friends, because all [Mysteries] which I heard from my Father I made known

[1] Literally, "come into being." In the archaic conception, nothing is created or happens through chance, but all things preëxist in a higher world; and whoever can act consciously in the world of causes can at will produce phenomenal results in the material world.

[2] Without the shining of the Sun there could be no fruitage, and this shining is attributed to the divine love. The Sun was conceived to be the abode of perfected souls, its light being due to their love for mortals; and as these Gods nourish men, so men should nourish the Gods by worship and libations.

to you. *You* did not choose me, but *I* chose *you;* and I gave you up,[1] that you may go away and bear fruit, and that your fruit may abide, so that whatsoever you may ask of the Father in my Name, he may give [it] to you. These things I command you, so that you may love one another.

"If the world hates *you*, you know that it has hated *me*, your First.[2] If you were of the world, the world would dearly love its own; but because you are not of the world, but *I* chose you out of the world, for this [reason] the world hates you. Bear in mind the saying which *I* told you, 'A slave is not greater than his Master.' If they hounded *me*, they will hound *you* also; if they have paid heed to my saying, they will also pay heed to yours. But all these [things] they will do to you on account of my Name, because they do not know him who sent me. If I had not come and spoken to them, they would not have had sin; but *now* they have no excuse concerning their sin.[3] He who hates *me* hates my Father also. If I had not done among them the works which no

---

[1] Gr. *theinai*, to put, set, establish; lay aside, give up— usually employed in the latter sense in this *Evangel*, as in "give up the ghost," "lays aside his outer garments," etc.

[2] See note 1, p. 84.

[3] Before a man's soul—his Logos—manifests in him, he is on the same plane of irresponsibility as the lower animals.

other one has done, they would not have had sin; but *now* they have seen [them], and have hated both *me* and my Father. But [it had to be], so that the saying may be fulfilled which was written in their Law:

" ' They hated me as a free gift.' [1]

Now, when the Advocate comes whom *I* shall send to you from the Father, that Breath of the Truth which goes forth from the Father, *he* will bear witness about me. Do *you*, also, bear witness, that you are[2] with me from a First-principle. These [words] I have spoken to you, so that you may not be made to trip. They will make you outcasts from the assembly; but an hour is coming, that every one who kills you will imagine that he is offering up a sacrifice to The God.[3] And they will do these [things] because they have no knowledge of the Father,

---

[1] Gr. *dôrea*, an honorary gift. The quotation is from the Greek of the *Septuagint*, *Ps.* xxxv. 19. Possibly the word may be used in an adverbial sense for "gratuitously," but more probably is here intended to express the ingratitude of men generally, as Iêsous calls himself the "free gift" in the incident of the Samareitan woman at the well.

[2] That is, "have existence."

[3] This sad prediction was only too literally fulfilled when in later days the murder of a "heretic" was "an act of faith" (*auto da fé*), and ignorant fanatics persecuted every one who dissented from their anthropomorphism and sarcolatry—their humanized God and carnalized Christ.

nor of me. But these [words] I have spoken
to you, so that when the hour[1] comes you may
call them to mind, that *I* said [them] to you.
But I did not say these [words] to you out of a
First-principle, because I was with you; but
now I am going to him who sent me. And not
one of you asks me, 'Where are you going?'
But because I have spoken these [words] to
you, pain has filled your heart. But *I* tell you
the Truth: it is to your interest that *I* should
go away, for if I do not go away the Advocate
will not come to you; but if I do go, I shall send
him to you; and, when he comes, *he* will
reproach the world about sin, and about right-
conduct, and about separation: about sin,
because they do not believe in *me;* and about
right-conduct, because I go to the Father, and
you no longer see me; and about separation,
because the Leader of this world has been
separated. I have yet many [things] to say to
you, but you can not prove[2] them now. But
when *he* has come—the Breath of the Truth—
he will show you the path[3] into the Whole Truth.

[1] The Vatican has, "the hour of them"; that is, "the time
for them."

[2] Gr. *bastazein,* to lift up, support; weigh in mind, consider, prove. The higher knowledge cannot be demonstrated
through the senses or by mere intellection, but only through
spiritual Seership, which is bestowed by the Paraklêtos.

[3] Gr. *hodêgein,* to show the way or path; to guide.

For he will not speak from himself, but whatever [words] he hears he will speak, and he will bring messages to you of the [things] coming.[1] *He* is about to make *me* Radiant,[2] because he will take of what is mine, and will bring [it] as a message to you. All [things] which the Father has are mine; for this [reason] I said that he takes of what is mine, and will bring it as a message to you.[3] A little while, and you do not see me; and again a little while, and you will see me—because I am going to the Father."

[Some] of his pupils, therefore, said one to another:

"What is this [enigma] that he says to us,

[1] Mere psychic prevision of coming events is not here intended, but the unveiling of the spiritual future of man, the Paraklêtos being the mediator between man and his inner God.

[2] That is, at the crucifixion. The action of the Paraklêtos produces a sun-like radiance about the head of the Initiate, represented in art as the aureole. See note 1, p. 131.

[3] The Sinaitic omits this sentence, apparently through mere carelessness in copying, the copyist mistaking the last words of the sentence for the same words in the sentence preceding it. A number of omissions from this cause are noticeable in the manuscripts, indicating that they were rarely proof-read, as they would have been by those who attached importance to the purity of the text, but were probably made by those who placed small value on their contents.

'A little while, and you do not see me; and again a little while, and you will see me'; and, 'Because I am going to the Father'?"

They kept on saying, therefore:

"What *is* this [enigma] that he says, that 'little while'? We do not know what he is speaking."

Iêsous knew that they desired to ask him, and said to them:

"Are you questioning one with another about this [saying], because I said, 'A little while, and you do not see me; and again a little while, and you will see me'? Amên, Amên, I say to you, *You* will wail and lament, but the world will rejoice. *You* will be pained, but your pain will be turned into joy. The woman, when she is bringing forth, has pain, because her hour has come; but when she has borne the child, she no longer thinks of the distress, because of the joy that a man [1] is born into the

---

[1] A new-born babe can hardly be called a "man," except in the generic sense as a "human being"; but here the birth "from above" is meant, the "man" being the sidereal body, and the "woman" the "virgin mother" or ether in the brain. The *Apokalypse* has the same allegory (xii. 1, 2): "And a great symbol (*sêmeion*) was seen in the Sky—a woman veiled with the Sun, and the Moon under her feet, and upon her head a crown of twelve stars; and being pregnant she cries out, in the pangs of child-birth, racked with pain to bring forth."

world. And *you* now indeed have pain; but again I shall see you, and your heart will rejoice, and your joy no one takes away from you. And in that day you shall ask *me* nothing. Amên, Amên, I say to you, Whatsoever you may ask of the Father in my Name, he will give you. Till now you have asked nothing in my Name; ask, and you shall receive, so that your joy may be made full. These [things] I have spoken to you in commonplaces; an hour is coming when I shall speak to you no longer in commonplaces, but shall openly bring you messages about the Father. In that day you will ask in my Name; and I do not say to you that *I* shall ask the Father about you, for the Father himself dearly loves you, because *you* have dearly loved *me*, and have believed that *I* came forth from The God.[1] I came forth from the Father, and have come into the world; again I give up the world, and am going to the Father."

His pupils say to him:

"See, *now* y o u are speaking openly, and saying no commonplace at all! *Now* we know that y o u know all [thoughts], and have no need that any one should *ask* y o u; by this [sign] we believe that y o u came forth from a God."

---

[1] The Vatican has, "from the Father."

Iêsous answered them:

"Do you believe [it] *now*? Behold, an hour is coming, and is now come, that you will be scattered, every one to his own [things], and will leave *me* alone; and [yet] I am not alone, because the Father is with me. These [words] I have spoken to you, so that in *me* you may have peace. In the world you have distress[1]; but take courage! *I* have conquered the world."[2]

These [words] Iêsous spoke; and he lifted up his eyes to the Sky, and said:

"Father, the hour is come. Make y o u r Son Radiant, so that the Son also may make y o u Radiant; even as y o u gave him authority over all flesh, so that all that you have given to him, he may give to them On-going Life. And this is the On-going Life, that they know y o u, the only true God, and him whom y o u sent, Anointed Iêsous.[3] *I* made *y o u* Radiant in the Earth, I made perfect the work which y o u have

[1] As the woman in child-birth has distress. All pain and sorrow in the material world are for the final emancipation of the soul, and therefore correspond to the pangs of birth.

[2] Every purified man or Initiate "conquers the world" by conquering the material elements of his own nature, the instincts, passions, etc.

[3] Only through the realization of the divine principle in one's self can union with Deity be attained, and the soul be freed from the succession of birth and death.

given me to do; and *now*, O Father, do *y o u* make *me* Radiant with yourself, in the Radiance which I had before this, when the world *was* with y o u.[1] I made y o u r Name shine forth to the men whom y o u have given me out of the world. They were y o u r s, and y o u have given them to me, and they have paid heed to y o u r saying. *Now* they know that *all* [things] which y o u gave to me are from *y o u*, because the words which y o u gave to me I have given to them, and they themselves received them, and knew truly that I came forth from y o u, and believed that *y o u* sent me. *I* entreat about them; I do not entreat about the world, but about those whom y o u have given me, because they are y o u r s, and all [things] which are mine are y o u r s, and y o u r s mine, and I have been made Radiant in them. And I am no longer in the world, and these [pupils] are in the world, and *I* am coming to *y o u.* Holy Father, preserve them in y o u r Name by which y o u have given [them] to me,[2] that they may be One, as *we* are. When I was with them, *I* preserved them in y o u r Name by which y o u have given [them] to me, and I guarded them, and not one out of them was lost except the

[1] That is, before the kosmos became separated or differentiated from the One, the divine unity.

[2] Here, and in the sentence following, the construction may possibly be, "y o u r Name which y o u have given me."

Son of the Loss, that the writing may be fulfilled.[2] But now I am coming to y o u, and these
[words] I speak in the world, that they may
have this joy of mine made full in them. *I*
have given them y o u r Thought, and the world
has hated them, because they are not of the
world, even as *I* am not of the world. I do not
entreat that y o u should take them out of the
world, but that y o u should preserve them from
the useless [function].[3] They are not of the
world, even as *I* am not of the world. Purify
them in the Truth[4]; y o u r Thought is Truth.
Even as y o u sent *me* into the world, so *I* also
sent them into the world, and on their account
I purify myself, so that *they* also may be purified
in Truth. And not about these only do I

---

[1] That is, Ioudas, the personification of sex.

[2] This does not refer to any particular passage in the *Old
Testament*, but only in a general way to the fall into generation. Ioudas, in the series of the Twelve, corresponds to the
zodiacal sign *Scorpio*, as does also Dan among the twelve
tribes. "Dan shall become a Serpent upon the Path, a
viper upon the highway" (*Gen.* xlix. 17). *Scorpio* is the
sign of the organs of reproduction; it is the house of Mars,
the garden-god. With the Akkadai, or race who preceded
the Chaldæans, it was represented as the Scorpion-monster
of darkness, which stings to death, yet guards and reproduces
the evening sun.

[3] That is, *sex*, the Serpent (theologically the Devil, or
"evil one") that wrought the "fall" of mankind.

[4] A reading of equal authority is, "y o u r Truth."

entreat, but also about those who through their saying believe in me, so that all [men] may be one; even as *y o u*, Father, [are] in me, and *I* in *y o u*, that *they* also may be one in us, so that the world may believe that *y o u* sent me. And the Radiance which y o u have given to me, *I* have given to them, that they may be one, even as *we* are one: *I* in *them*, and *y o u* in *me*, that they may be made perfect in one; so that the world may know that *y o u* sent me, and loved them even as y o u loved me. Father, those whom y o u have given to me, I will that where *I* am, *they* also may be with me, so that they may see this Radiance of mine which y o u gave me because y o u loved me before [the] casting-down[1] of [the] world. Just Father, the world, indeed, did not know y o u, but *I* knew y o u, and these [pupils] knew that *y o u* sent me; and I made known to them y o u r Name, and I shall make [it] known, so that the love with which y o u loved me may be in them, and *I* in them."

Having said these [things], Iêsous went out with his pupils to the other side of the torrent

---

[1] Gr. *katabolé*, a throwing down; laying down (a foundation). Ôrigenês says that in the *New Testament* usage of this word it relates to the descent of the souls from the higher to the lower spheres. According to his teaching, the souls sinned before the material world existed, and they are condemned to migrate from body to body (reincarnate) until purified.

of the Cedars, where there was a garden,[1] into which he himself entered, and his pupils. Now, *Ioudas* also, who was delivering him up, knew the place, because Iêsous had often resorted there with his pupils. Ioudas, therefore, having received the company of soldiers,[2] and retainers from the archpriests and Pharisaians, comes there with lights and torches and weapons.[3] Iêsous, therefore, knowing all the [things] that were coming upon him, went out and said to them:

"Whom do you seek?"

They answered him:

"Iêsous the Nazôraian."

Iêsous said to them:

"*I* am [he]."

Now, Ioudas also, who was delivering him up, was standing with them. When, therefore, he said to them, "*I* am [he]," they retired backward, and fell to the ground. Again, therefore, he put the question to them:

"Whom do you seek?"

---

[1] The "gardens" in the narrative are symbolical, like the "garden in Eden," and represent the force-centres through which the Paraklêtos acts.

[2] Gr. *speira*, a body of men-at-arms. But the primary meaning of the word is "a spiral," "a coil," and here it is a word-play referring to the spiral Fire of the Paraklêtos—called in Sanskrit the *kundalini*, or "coiled-up" force.

[3] Or, "an armed force," "men-at-arms."

And they said:

"Iêsous the Nazôraian."

Iêsous answered:

"I told you that *I* am [he]. If, therefore, you seek *me*, let these [pupils] go their way."

[This was said] so that the saying might be fulfilled which he said, "Whom y o u have given to me, not one of them did I lose."

Then Simôn Petros, having a knife,[1] drew it, and struck the Archpriest's slave, and cut off his right ear-tip.[2] Now, the slave's name was Malchos. Iêsous, therefore, said to Petros:

"Put that knife into the sheath. The cup which the Father has given me, shall I not drink it?"

The company of soldiers, therefore, and the commander,[3] and the retainers of the Ioudaians, arrested Iêsous and bound him, and led him to Annas first, for he was father-in-law of Kaiaphas, who was Archpriest of that year. Now, it was Kaiaphas who had advised the Ioudaians that it was to their interest that one

[1] Gr. *machaira*, a large knife, dagger, short sword; properly a hunting-knife, and not a soldier's weapon.

[2] Gr. *ôtion*, a little ear. The ear-tip is probably meant. The constant use of diminutive forms in this *Evangel* is peculiar.

[3] Gr. *chiliarchos*, commander of a thousand men; here, the commander of a Roman cohort, or body of five or six hundred soldiers.

man should die because of the common people. Now, there went along with Iêsous Simôn Petros and another pupil; and that pupil was known to the Archpriest, and went in with Iêsous into the court of the Archpriest, but Petros stood at the door, outside. This other pupil, therefore, who was known to the Archpriest, went out and spoke to the woman who kept the door, and brought in Petros. This slave-girl, therefore, who kept the door, says to Petros:

"Are *y o u* also [one] of this man's pupils?"

He says:

"I am not."

Now, the slaves and the retainers were standing there, having made a charcoal fire, because it was cold, and they were warming themselves; and Petros also was with them, standing and warming himself. The Archpriest, therefore, asked Iêsous about his pupils and about his teaching. Iêsous answered him:

"*I* have spoken openly to the world; *I* taught every time in an assembly, and in the temple-courts where all the Ioudaians meet; and in secret I spoke nothing. Why do *y o u* ask *me?* Ask those who have heard what I spoke to them; see, these [men] know what *I* said."

Now, when he had said these [words], one of the retainers, who was standing by, gave Iêsous a slap, saying:

" Do y o u answer the Archpriest in that way ? "

Iêsous answered him :

" If I spoke badly,[1] bear witness about what was bad; but if rightly, why do y o u beat me [2]? "

Annas sent him bound to Kaiaphas, the Archpriest.

Now, Simôn Petros was standing and warming himself. They said, therefore, to him :

" Are y o u also [one] of his pupils ? "

He denied [it], and said :

" I am not."

Says one of the slaves of the Archpriest, being a relative of him whose ear-tip Petros had cut off :

" Did not *I* see y o u in the garden with him ? "

Again, therefore, Petros denied [it], and immediately a cock crew.

They conduct Iêsous, therefore, from Kaiaphas to the court-house. And it was early in the morning, and they themselves did not go into the court-house, that they might not be polluted, but might eat the " Passing-over."[3]

---

[1] Gr. *kakôs*, wrongly, improperly; rudely, insolently.

[2] Literally, "give me a hiding." (Gr. *derein*, to skin, flay, remove the hide; colloquially, to thrash, cudgel.)

[3] Yet Iêsous and his pupils had already eaten it, according to the Synoptists, who thus fix the date of the crucifixion

Pilatos, therefore, went out to them, and said:

"What charge do you bring against this man?"

They answered and said to him:

"If this [man] were not a wrong-doer, we would not have delivered him up to y o u."

Pilatos, therefore, said to them:

"Take him yourselves, and judge him according to your Law."

The Ioudaians said to him:

"*We* are not allowed to kill any one."

[This was said] so that the saying of Iêsous might be fulfilled which he said, showing by a sign by what kind of death he was about to die.

Pilatos, therefore, went back into the courthouse, and called Iêsous, and said to him:

"Are *y o u* the 'Ruler of the Ioudaians'?"

Iêsous answered:

on the 15th day of the month Nisan; whereas the account in this *Evangel* places the "last supper" on the evening *before*, making the crucifixion take place on the 14th Nisan. Harmonists and commentators have exhausted their ingenuity in vainly attempting to reconcile the two accounts. Mystically, however, there is no discrepancy; for in this *Evangel* Iêsous is himself the paschal Lamb, and the crucifixion is the "Passing-over," to which the "last supper" is merely preparatory. The allegory in the Synoptics relates to the lower planes—material, psychic, and sidereal— whereas that of Iôannês is purely spiritual, being that of the Seer, the fourth degree of Initiation (*epopteia*).

"Do *y o u* say this [charge] from yourself, or did others tell y o u about me?"

Pilatos answered:

"Am *I* a Ioudaian?[1]   Yo u r own class and the archpriests have delivered y o u up to me. What was it y o u did?"

Iêsous answered:

"This 'Ruling'[2] of mine is not of this world. If *my* Ruling were of this world, my retainers would strive that I should not be given up to the Ioudaians; but *now* this Ruling of mine is not from this place."[3]

Pilatos, therefore, said to him:

"Are *y o u* not therefore a Ruler?"

Iêsous answered:

"It is *y o u* who say that *I* am a Ruler.[4]   To this [end] *I* have been born,[5] and to this [end] I have come into the world, that I may bear witness to the Truth.   Every one who is of the Truth hears my voice."

Pilatos says to him:

---

[1] Or, "Surely *I* am not a Ioudaian."

[2] See note 3, p. 94.

[3] That is, not until after the apotheosis of the crucifixion.

[4] Or, "It is *y o u* who say, '*I* am a Ruler.'"

[5] Iêsous speaks here as the Logos, which "became flesh"; this birth, or "coming into being," is the descending from the noumenal world, the Truth, into the phenomenal world or sphere of transition; and from the latter he came into the kosmos or outer world.

"What is 'truth'[1]?"

And having said this, he went out again to the Ioudaians, and says to them:

"*I* do not find any guilt in him. But there is a custom of yours that I should release to you one [prisoner] at the 'Passing-over.' Is it your will, therefore, that I should release to you this 'Ruler of the Ioudaians'?"

Then they all cried back, saying:

"Not this [man], but Barabbas!"

Now, this Barabbas was a bandit. Pilatos, therefore, took Iêsous and flogged him. And the soldiers, having twined a crown of thorns, put [it] on his head, and threw round him a purple mantle. And they kept coming up to him and saying, "Hail, 'Ruler of the Ioudaians'!" and giving him slaps. And Pilatos went outside again, and says to them:

"See, I am bringing him outside to you, so that you may know that I find no guilt in him."

Iêsous, therefore, came outside, wearing the thorny crown and the purple mantle. And [Pilatos] says to them:

"See, [this is] the Man."[2]

---

[1] Pilatos uses the word tritely; throughout the dialogue he is shown to be unconscious of any inner meaning in the words of Iêsous.

[2] The Vatican reads "a man." Pilatos was apparently trying to awaken a sense of pity in the mob by thus ex-

When, therefore, the archpriests and the retainers saw him, they cried out, saying:

"Crucify [him], crucify him!"

Pilatos says to them:

"Take him and crucify [him] yourselves, for *I* do not find any guilt in him."

The Ioudaians answered him:

"*We* have a Law, and according to our Law he is bound to die, because he made himself a Son of a God."[1]

When, therefore, Pilatos heard this saying, he was more dismayed, and he went back into the court-house, and says to Iêsous:

"From what place are *y o u?*"

But Iêsous gave him no answer. Pilatos, therefore, says to him:

"Do y o u not speak to *me?* Do y o u not know that I have authority to release y o u, and have authority to crucify y o u?"

Iêsous answered him:

"Y o u would have no authority against me if it had not been given y o u from above[2]; for

hibiting Iêsous to them; and the cruel fanaticism of the priest-caste is forcibly contrasted with the justice and mercy displayed by the rough Roman military commander.

[1] *Lev.* xxiv. 16.

[2] The words have an inner meaning; for Pilatos was not only free from personal responsibility by virtue of his office, but also, against his own will, was an instrument in the hands of Destiny.

this [reason] he who delivered me up to y o u has a greater sin."

From this [time] Pilatos sought to release him; but the Ioudaians cried out, saying:

"If y o u release this [man] y o u are no friend of Kaisar's.[1] Every one who makes himself a Ruler declares himself against Kaisar."

Pilatos, therefore, having heard this saying, brought Iêsous outside, and took his seat on the raised platform in a place called "Stone-laid,"[2] but in Hebrew *Gabbatha*. Now, it was "Preparation"[3] for the "Passing-over," and it was about the sixth hour. And he says to the Ioudaians:

"See, [this is] your Ruler."

But *they* cried out:

"Away, away [with him]! Crucify him!"

Pilatos says to them:

"Shall I crucify your *Ruler?*"

The archpriests answered:

---

[1] The Greek form of the Latin "Cæsar."

[2] Gr. *lithostrôtos*, inlaid with stones. Psycho-physiologically, the spinal column is here meant, the "raised platform" being the atlas, whence the Fire of the Paraklêtos passes through the foramen into the cranium, manifesting the seventh of the magnetic colors, which correspond respectively to the seven centres of the spinal cord. Therefore, in the sentence following, it is said to be "about the sixth hour," and the "preparation for the passing-over."

[3] Gr. *paraskeuê*, a getting ready.

"We have no Ruler except Kaisar."

Then, therefore, he delivered him up to them to be crucified. And they took Iêsous and led him off. And he, carrying the cross for himself, went out to the place called "Skull," which in Hebrew is called *Golgotha,*[1] where they crucified him, and with him two others, on the one side and on the other side, and Iêsous in

---

[1] Gr. *kranion,* Heb. *golgotha,* Lat. *calvaria,* Eng. "skull." The "crucifixion" takes place in the brain. The Fire, or electric force, rises to the vertex of the skull, where is the opening called mystically the "door of Iêsous" (*thura tou Iêsou*); at the highest centre in the brain, called the "third eye" (the *conarium* of the anatomists), it is intersected by the Water, or magnetic force, forming a cross in the brain. The strain of the two forces at the point of intersection throws out a spiral, which coils about the head. The physical body is then in a deep trance, seemingly dead, and the consciousness is in the sidereal body. The man is thus "born from above," "born of Water and of Breath"; but this is possible only for the purified ascetic who has reached the androgynous state and is thus "Self-born" (*monogenês*). This noëtic action in the brain of the Seer is expressed by the symbol ⊕ ; that of the ordinary man being ⊖, and of the woman ⊕. In this sacred trance the light about the head has the appearance of a sun; hence the aureole and cross shown about the head of Iêsous. The "thorny crown," of a golden color, represents the radiation of the Fire; and the "purple mantle," the hue which the Radiance (*doxa*) takes from the magnetic force or Water. See Appendix II., "The Birth from Above." The "crucifixion" is an allegory of spiritual regeneration, not an historical record of a physical death.

the middle.[1]   And Pilatos wrote also a title[2]
and put [it] on the cross; and what was written
was, "Iêsous the Nazôraian, the Ruler of the
Ioudaians."   This title, therefore, many of the
Ioudaians read, because the place of the city
where Iêsous was crucified was close by, and it
was written in Hebrew, in Greek, [and] in
Latin.   The archpriests of the Ioudaians,
therefore, said to Pilatos:

"Do not write 'The Ruler of the Ioudaians,'
but '*He* said, "I am Ruler of the Ioudaians."'"

Pilatos answered:

"What I have written, I have written."

The soldiers, therefore, when they had
crucified Iêsous, took his outer garments, and
made four shares, for each soldier a share; also
[they took] the inner garment.[3] Now, the
inner garment was without seam, being woven
from those above[4] through the whole.   They
said, therefore, to each other:

---

[1] The "two others" symbolize the positive and negative
forces which go with the Fire, as the latter passes through
the central tube of the spinal cord.

[2] Gr. *titlos* (answering to the Latin *titlus*), a technical
Roman term for an inscription giving the cause of a
malefactor's condemnation.

[3] Gr. *chitôn*, a woollen frock worn next the body.

[4] The expression is peculiar, a play upon words. As
applied to the woollen frock it would mean that it had been
made on a hand-loom from the top through its whole length;

"Let us not divide it, but draw lots for it, whose it shall be."

[This was said] so that the writing might be fulfilled, which says:

"They shared my outer garments among themselves,

And upon my raiment they tossed up a die."[1]

The soldiers, therefore, did these [things].

Now, there were standing by the cross of Iêsous his mother and his mother's sister, Mariam, the [mother] of Klôpas,[2] and Mariam the Magdalian.[3] Iêsous, therefore, seeing his

---

but allegorically it refers to the impartible ether in the brain, which is non-molecular. The aureole, or "outer garments," is divided by the cross into four parts, and is frequently so depicted in mediæval art.

[1] *Ps.* xxii. 18. The lot, or die (*klêros*), was a potsherd or pebble used in sortilege.

[2] The Greek leaves the relationship uncertain; Mariam may have been the wife of Klôpas, but more probably the name Klôpas is an equivalent for Iakôbos (James), the words being similar in meaning (Iakôb, supplanter; Klôpas, one who is stealthy), and in the Synoptics Mariam is called the mother of Iakôbos (*Matt.* xxvii. 56; *Mk.* xv. 40).

[3] Gr. *magdalênê*, a [woman] of Magdala; one of the temple-women (sacred prostitutes). There was a temple at Magdala, on the western coast of the Lake of Tiberias; but the place had its name from the temple or "tower of God," so that whether *magdalênê* be taken to mean "temple-woman" or "of Magdala," the significance is the same.

mother, and that pupil standing by whom he loved, says to his mother:

"[Good] woman, see, [this is] y o u r son."

Then he says to the pupil:

"See, [this is] y o u r mother."

And from that hour the pupil took her to his own [home].[1] After this [bequest], Iêsous, knowing that all [things] had now been made perfect, so that the writing might be made perfect, says:

"I thirst."[2]

Now, there was set a vessel full of sour wine. Having, therefore, put a sponge full of the sour wine on a hyssop-stalk, they brought [it] to his mouth. When, therefore, Iêsous had received the sour wine, he said:

"It is made perfect."

And inclining his head, he gave up the Breath.

The Ioudaians, therefore, since it was "Preparation," so that the bodies should not remain on the cross in the Sabbath—for the day was a great [one] of that Sabbath—asked Pilatos that their legs might be broken, and

---

[1] Iôannês is here made the successor of Iêsous, just as Iôannês the Lustrator is his predecessor. Mystically, the three are one, a literal "trinity in unity."

[2] *Ps.* xxii. 15; lxix. 21. The Psalms were originally hymns of Initiation. Quotations such as the above seem to refer to Initiation-formulas rather than to prophecies.

they might be taken away. The soldiers, therefore, came; and they did, indeed, break the
legs of the first, and of that other[1] who was
crucified with him. But on coming to Iêsous,
when they saw him already dead, they did not
break his legs; but one of the soldiers pierced
his side with a spear, and immediately there
came out blood and water. And he who saw
[it] has borne witness, and his witness is true;
and *he* knows that he is saying a true [thing],
so that *you* also may believe. For these
[things] came about so that the writing might
be fulfilled:

"Not a bone of his shall be broken."[2]

And again another writing says:

"They shall look on him whom they pierced."[3]

Now, after these [events], Iôsêph of Arima-
thaia, being a pupil of Iêsous—but in secret,
through his fear of the Ioudaians—asked
Pilatos that he might take away the body of
Iêsous; and Pilatos permitted [him]. He came,

---

[1] Namely, that one who went with him to Paradise (*Lk.*
xxiii. 43). The positive (solar) force ascends with the Fire
of the Paraklêtos into the brain, while the negative (lunar)
force stops at its base. Similarly in the *Apokalypse* the
"woman veiled with the *Sun*" has the *Moon* "under her
feet" (see note 1, p. 185).

[2] *Ps.* xxxiv. 20.

[3] *Zech.* xii. 10.

therefore, and took away the body of Iêsous.
And there came also Nikodêmos—he who had
come to him by night at the first—bringing a
mixture of myrrh and aloes, about a hundred
pounds. Then they took the body of Iêsous
and swathed it with linen bandages with the
aromatics, as the custom is with the Ioudaians
to prepare for entombing. Now, in the place
where he was crucified there was a garden, and
in the garden a new tomb, in which no one as
yet was laid. There, then, because of the
Ioudaians' "Preparation," as the tomb was near
at hand, they laid Iêsous.

Now, on the first [day] of the Sabbath,[1]
Mariam the Magdalian comes early, while it is
yet dark, to the tomb, and sees that the stone is
taken away from the tomb. She runs, therefore, and comes to Simôn Petros and to that
other pupil whom Iêsous dearly loved, and says
to them:
"They have taken away the Master out of the
tomb, and we do not know where they have laid
him."
Petros, therefore, went out, and the other
pupil, and they were coming to the tomb.
Now, the two ran together, and the other pupil
outran Petros and came first to the tomb, and

[1] See note 1, p. 110.

stooping to peer in, he sees the linen bandages lying; however, he did not go in. Simôn Petros, therefore, comes also, following him closely, and went into the tomb; and he observes the linen bandages lying, and the handkerchief that had been on his head not lying with the linen bandages, but by itself, rolled up, in one place. Then, therefore, the other pupil also— he who came first to the tomb—went in; and he saw, and believed [Mariam's report]. For as yet they did not know the writing, that he must rise up from among the dead ones. The pupils, therefore, went away again by themselves.

But Mariam kept standing outside at the tomb, weeping. While, therefore, she was weeping, she stooped to peer into the tomb, and sees two Messengers in white sitting, one at the head, and one at the feet, where the body of Iêsous had been lying. And *they* say to her:

"[Good] woman, why are y o u weeping?"

She says to them:

"Because they have taken away my Master, and I do not know where they have laid him."

Having said these [words], she turned to the [things] that lay behind, and sees Iêsous standing, and she did not know that it was Iêsous. Iêsous said to her:

"[Good] woman, why are y o u weeping? Whom do y o u seek?"

She, thinking that it is the gardener, says to him:

"Master, if *y o u* carried him off, tell me where y o u laid him, and *I* will take him away."

Iêsous says to her:

"Mariam!"

She, having turned, says to him in Hebrew:

"*Rabbouni!*" (that is to say, "Teacher.")

Iêsous says to her:

"Do not try to touch me, for I have not yet gone up to my Father; but go to my brothers and say to them, 'I am going up to my Father and your Father, and my God and your God.'"

Mariam the Magdalian comes and brings a message to the pupils that she had seen the Master, and he had said these [words] to her.

When, therefore, it was evening of that first day of the Sabbath, and the doors having been shut where the pupils were assembled, through fear of the Ioudaians, Iêsous came and stood before all,[1] and says to them:

"Peace to you!"[2]

And having said this [greeting], he showed them his hands and his side. The pupils, therefore, rejoiced when they saw the Master. Iêsous, therefore, said to them again:

---

[1] The Greek idiom is, "in the midst."

[2] The common Eastern salutation, the *salâm.*

"Peace to you! As the Father has sent me, *I* also send you."

And having said this, he blew on [them],[1] and said to them:

"Receive [the] holy Breath. If you take away any one's sins, they *are* taken away; if you retain any one's, they *are* retained."[2]

But Thômas, one of the Twelve, he who was called "Twin," was not with them when Iêsous came. The other pupils, therefore, said to him:

"We have seen the Master."

But *he* said to them:

---

[1] Gr. *emphusan*, to inflate (as a bladder), to puff up. The Beza has, *insuflavit in eos*. The expression appears absurd if understood as relating to the lung-breath; but here it refers to the Paraklêtos, "the Breath of the Truth."

[2] The text here is corrupt and uncertain, the manuscripts having various readings. The general meaning, however, is sufficiently clear, and accords with the teaching of Paulos (I. *Cor*. v. 12–vi. 3): "For what [is it] to *me* to judge the exotericists? Do not *you* judge the esotericists? But The God judges the exotericists. Remove the useless [man] from among yourselves. Does any one of you who has trouble in relation to another dare bring it to trial before unjust [men] and not before holy [men]? Do you not know that the holy [men] will judge the world; and if the world is to be brought to trial by you, are you not worthy of the very little matters of judgment? Do you not know that we are to judge Messengers—why not, then, the affairs of this life?"

"Unless I see on his hands the print of the nails, and put my finger into the print of the nails, and put my hand into his side, I shall not believe [it] at all."

And after eight days his pupils were again within, and Thômas with them. Iêsous comes, the doors having been shut, and stood before all, and said:

"Peace to you!"

Afterwards he says to Thômas:

"Reach y o u r finger here, and see my hands; and reach y o u r hand [here], and put [it] into my side; and be no longer an unbeliever, but a believer."

Thômas answered and said to him:

"My Master and my God!"

Iêsous says to him:

"Because y o u have seen me, y o u have believed. Immortal [are] they who have not seen [me] and [yet] have believed!"[1]

Many other[2] signs then indeed Iêsous did in the presence of his pupils, which are not written in this book[3]; but these [things] have been written, that you may believe that Iêsous is the

[1] According to mystical philosophy, all sense-impressions are illusionary, and knowledge of the realities of life, the *noumena*, can be derived only from the spiritual consciousness.

[2] In the Greek idiom, "Many and other."

[3] Gr. *biblion* (diminutive from *biblos*), a book, tablet, scroll.

Anointed, the Son of The God, and that, believing, you may have Life in his Name.[1]

After these [events] Iêsous made himself shine forth again to his pupils on the Sea of Tiberias, and he shone forth in this manner. There were together Simôn Petros, and Thômas who is called "Twin," and Nathanaêl from Kana of Galilaia, and the [sons] of Zebedaios, and two others of his pupils.   Simôn Petros says to them:

"I am going off to fish."

They say to him:

"*We* also are coming with you."

They went out and got into the boat immediately, and during that night they took nothing.   But when it was already becoming early morning, Iêsous stood on the beach.

---

[1] As this is apparently a formal ending to the *Evangel*, a majority of the critics regard the portion following it as a later addition either by the same or another hand; but the evidence in favor of this theory is anything but conclusive. The closing passage, giving an account of the third appearance of Iêsous to his pupils after his crucifixion, is found in all the ancient manuscripts, and there are no sound reasons for questioning its genuineness.   In fact, the supposed formal ending merely marks the close of the psycho-physiological reading of the allegory; and all that follows it is historically prophetic, foretelling the fate of the Christian Church, its conversion into a political tool, and its loss of the esoteric doctrine.

The pupils, however, did not know that it was Iêsous. Iêsous, therefore, says to them:

"Boys, have you anything to eat?"[1]

They answered him:

"No."

And he said to them:

"Cast the net into the parts to the right of the boat, and you will find [fish]."

They cast, therefore, and no longer were able to draw it from[2] the multitude of the fishes. That pupil, therefore, whom Iêsous loved, says to Petros:

"It is the Master."

Simôn Petros, therefore, when he heard that it was the Master, girded on his blouse—for he was lightly clad—and threw himself into the sea.[3] But the other pupils came in the small-boat—for they were not far from the land, but about two hundred arm-lengths[4] off—dragging the net [full] of the fishes. When, therefore,

---

[1] Gr. *prosphagion*, a relish, something eaten with other food; here it is applied to fish. The sentence is in colloquial Greek, employing the expression commonly used in asking fishers or hunters if they had any game.

[2] Literally, "away from."

[3] That is, being in haste to reach the Master. He was in his under-garment only, the word *gumnos*, "stripped," being applied in common language to one having on only the *chitôn*, or woollen frock.

[4] Gr. *pechus*, elbow; the length of the arm from the point of the elbow to the tip of the little finger; a cubit.

they got out on the land, they see a charcoal fire set, and a small fish laid on it, and a loaf of bread. Iêsous says to them:

"Bring [some] from the small fishes which you just now took."

Simôn Petros, therefore, went on board and drew the net to the land, full of big fishes, a hundred and fifty-three; and though there were so many, the net was not torn. Iêsous says to them:

"Come, breakfast."

And not one of the pupils dared to inquire of him, "Who are *you?*" knowing that it was the Master. Iêsous comes and takes the loaf of bread, and gives [it] to them, and the fish likewise. This was now the third [time] Iêsous shone forth to his pupils after he had risen up from among the dead ones. When, therefore, they had breakfasted, Iêsous says to Simôn Petros:

"Simôn, [son] of Iônas, do *you* love[1] me more than these [fellow-pupils]?"

[1] Gr. *agapan* (primary meaning, "to hug"), to receive willingly; to hold in esteem. It denotes love that arises from regard or veneration; whereas *philein* (here rendered "to love dearly") refers to love of the emotional sort, fondness, affection. The use of the two words in the above dialogue is inimitable, and cannot be preserved in a literal translation. Paraphrased, it would run about as follows: "Simôn, do *you* esteem me more highly than *you* do *your*

He says to him:

"Yes, Master. *You* know that I dearly love
y o u."

He says to him:

"Feed my lambs."[1]

He says to him again a second time:

"Simôn, [son] of Iônas, do y o u love
me?"

He says to him:

"Yes, Master. *You* know that I dearly love
y o u."

He says to him:

"Shepherd my sheep."

He says to him the third time:

"Simôn, [son] of Iônas, do y o u 'dearly love'
me?"

Petros was grieved because he said to him
the third time, "Do y o u 'dearly love' me?"
and he says to him:

"Master, *y o u* know all [things]; *y o u* well
know that I dearly love y o u."

Iêsous says to him:

"Feed my sheep. Amên, Amên, I say to
y o u, When y o u were younger y o u used to gird
yourself, and walk where y o u willed; but when
y o u have grown aged y o u will stretch out y o u r

fellow-pupils?" "Yes, Master; *y o u* know that I am very
fond of y o u."

[1] The Vatican has "lambkins," and the Beza "sheep."

hands, and another will gird y o u and carry
y o u where y o u do not will [to go]."

Now, he said this [similitude], showing by a
sign by what kind of death he should make
Radiant The God. And when he had said this,
he says to him:

"Follow me."

Petros, turning around, sees the pupil whom
Iêsous loved following—the one who leaned
back on his breast at the dinner, and said,
"Master, who is it that is about to deliver y o u
up?" Petros, therefore, when he saw this
[pupil], says to Iêsous:

"Master, and what of this [one]?"

Iêsous says to him:

"If I will that he abide until I come, what
[is that] to *y o u?*[1] Come *y o u* with me."

This saying, therefore, went forth to the
brothers, "That pupil is not to die"; but Iêsous
did not say to him, "He is not to die," but, "If
I will that he abide until I come, what [is that]
to *y o u?*" This is the pupil who both bears
witness about these [things], and has written

---

[1] Petros, who three times denied his Master, yet three
times asserted his love for him, typifies the Church, which,
esoteric in its earlier days, was later made an instrument of
the civil government and suffered death, that is, became exoteric; while Iôannês, the beloved pupil, who abides till the
coming of the Master, is a type of the esoteric knowledge
that endures even though religions perish.

these [things]; and we know that his witness is true. But there are ever so many other [things] which Iêsous did, which if they are written one by one, I suppose that the world itself will not contain the books that are being written [about them]. [1]

[1] So literally in the Greek; but the Authorized Version and Revised Version modify the exaggeration by construing, "the books that should be written."

APPENDICES

APPENDIX I.

THE PRODIGAL SON.

Luke xv. 11–32.

A CERTAIN man had two sons. And the younger of them said to the Father:

"Father, give me the share of the Substance [1] that falls to me."

And he divided the Living [2] between them. And not many days after, the younger son, when he had gathered all together, took a journey to a far-distant country, [3] and there he scattered abroad [4] his Substance, living unsav-

---

[1] Gr. *ousia*, being, essence, the divine substance intermediate between the Absolute Deity and the objective Universe, the efficient cause of all phenomenal manifestation; substance, property. In the literal sense, the Son receives his share of the property; but allegorically he is the Soul going outward into the manifested worlds.

[2] Gr. *bios*, life; means of living

[3] Gr. *chôra*, a space, place; tract, region, land, country. See note 3, p. 105.

[4] The forces of the soul are diffused as it manifests in Time and Space.

ingly.[1] Now, when he had spent his all, there came about a mighty famine throughout that country, and he himself began to be in want.[2] And he passed over[3] and joined himself to one of the citizens of that country; and he sent him into his fields to feed pigs. And he longed[4] to fill his belly[5] with the carob-pods[6] which the pigs were eating; and no one gave to him. Now, when he came to himself,[7] he said:

" How many wage-workers of my Father have bread more than enough, but *I* here am perishing with hunger! I shall rise up[8] and cross over

[1] Gr. *asôtôs*, without saving, prodigally, profligately.

[2] Literally, "to fall short."

[3] In the primary sense, "was ferried across." He crossed the "river of generation" and incarnated in a physical body, becoming subject to its longings and desires, the "pigs."

[4] Gr. *epithumein*, to set one's desire upon; to covet, lust. The principle of desire, the vital impulse (*thumos*), has its seat in the midriff, according to the ancients.

[5] Gr. *koilia*, the stomach; the lower belly; the seat of the vital impulse (*epithumia*), the longing for sensation or thirst for physical existence.

[6] The fruit of the carob-tree. The pods, from their resemblance to the "locust," were popularly called "St. John's bread," with the notion that they constituted his food in the wilderness.

[7] At the outermost limit of its cycle, in the mire of physical existence, the Soul comes to self-consciousness, and then begins its homeward journey, its return to the "house of the Father."

[8] The technical expression for rising from the dead.

to my Father, and shall say to him, 'Father,
I have erred against the Sky[1] and in your
presence; no longer am I worthy to be called
your Son; make me as one of your wage-
workers.'"

And he rose up and went to his Father.
Now, while he was yet far away, his Father saw
him, and his heart was stirred, and he ran and
fell on his neck, and tenderly kissed him.
But the Son said to him:

"Father, I have erred against the Sky and
in your presence, and no longer am I worthy
to be called your Son; make me as one of
your wage-workers."[2]

But the Father said to his slaves:

"Bring forth quickly the first garment[3] and
put [it] on him, and give a seal-ring into his
hand,[4] and sandals to his feet; and bring forth
the fatted calf[5] and sacrifice [it]; and let us eat
and rejoice, because this my son was one dead
and is alive, was one lost and is found."

---

[1] Gr. *ouranos*, the vault of the sky considered as a super-
terrestrial globe upon which the Gods lived; also the ethereal
substance composing it.

[2] The last clause of this sentence is omitted in some manuscripts.

[3] The sidereal body (*sôma pneumatikon*) is here meant.

[4] Or, in the English idiom, "bestow upon him a seal-ring."

[5] Or, "young bull," such as was sacrificed to the Egyptian
God Apis.

And they began to rejoice. Now, his older Son was in the field, and as he was coming and drew near the house he heard a sound of music and a chorus of singers; and calling to him one of the slave-boys, he demanded what these [things] meant. And he said to him:

"Your brother is come, and your Father has sacrificed the fatted calf, because he has recovered him safe and hale."

And he was wrathful,[1] and was unwilling to go in. Then his Father went out and spoke to him; but he, answering, said to his Father:

"Behold, so many years have I slaved for you, and I never passed over a command of yours; and you never gave *me* a kid, so that I might rejoice with my friends. But when this your Son came, who has consumed your Living with prostitutes, you have sacrificed for him the fatted calf!"

And he said to him:

"Child, *you* are with me at all times, and all [things] that are mine are yours. Now, you ought to have rejoiced and been glad because this your brother was one dead and is alive, and was one lost and is found."

[1] Those Gods (unfallen Souls) who have not passed through the human stage of existence are usually represented as being jealous of the mortals; for the purified human Soul is superior to all the celestial beings who have never been incarnated. See note 2, p. 208.

APPENDIX II.

THE BIRTH FROM ABOVE.

I. *Cor.* xv. 35–56.

BUT some one will say, "How are the dead ones raised up, and with what sort of body do they come?"[1] Thoughtless one,[2] that which *you* sow is not made living unless it dies, and that which you sow, you do not sow the *body* which will come into being, but a naked grain, it may chance of wheat or of some other [kinds]; but The God gives it a body just as he has determined, and to each of the things sown its own proper body. All flesh is not the same flesh: but there is one [flesh] of men, another of

[1] The question is put literally, referring to those who are "dead" in the ordinary sense; but by a play upon the word the answer applies it to those who are prisoned in the physical body or "dead form."

[2] Gr. *aphrôn*, unintelligent, without sense (*phrên*). Psycho-physiologically, the lower intelligence (*phrên*) has its seat in the heart-region.

animals, another of fishes, and another of birds. And [there are] bodies of Sky-substance[1] and bodies of Earth-substance[2]; but [there is] a certain Radiance of those of Sky-substance, and a different [Radiance] of those of Earth-substance; one Radiance of the Sun, and another Radiance of the Moon, and another Radiance of the Stars[3]—for Star differs from Star in Radiance. Thus, also, is the Raising-up[4] of the dead ones. It is sown in a destroying, raised in indestructibility; sown in a disesteeming, raised in Radiance; sown in a weakening, raised in force; sown as a psychic body, raised as a Breath-body.[5] There is[6] a psychic body, and there is a Breath-body; hence it is written: " The first man, Adam, came into being in a psychic form "[7]; the last Adam, in a

---

[1] The pneumatic bodies (solar).

[2] The psychic bodies (lunar).

[3] The various hierarchies of ethereal beings.

[4] Gr. *anastasis.* See note 2, p. 112.

[5] The man whose only conscious life is in his physical body is said to be "dead"; but when the animal nature is subdued, the passions and desires destroyed, he becomes conscious of the psychic world, and the psychic senses awaken; renouncing the psychic powers, holding them to be of no enduring benefit (see note 3, p. 165), he is raised by the force (*dunamis*) of the Paraklêtos to the purely spiritual plane of being.

[6] The Vatican reads, "If there is."

[7] Gr. *psuchê,* the ethereal body or ghost (*Gen.* ii. 7).

life-producing Breath. Yet the Breath [body] was not first, but the psychic; afterwards, the Breath [body]. The first man is from the Earth, of dust[1]; the second man, the Master, is from the Sky. As that which is of dust, so also are they who are of dust; and as that which is of Sky-substance, so also are they who are of Sky-substance. And even as we have worn the likeness[2] of that which is of dust, we shall also wear the likeness of that which is of Sky-substance.[3] Now, I say this, brothers, Flesh and blood can not inherit the Realm of a God, nor does the destructible inherit the indestruc-

[1] Gr. *choïkos*, of loose earth or dust heaped up, of spore-dust, dust containing the seminal principle; here used metaphorically of the cosmic dust, or psychic substance. Unpurified men were termed "earthy ones" (*choïkoi*), as distinguished from the psychics *(psuchikoi)*, who had received the lustration of Water, and the spiritually re-born (*pneumatikoi*), who had received the lustration of the holy Breath. The term *hoi pistikoi* ("those having faith") was also applied to the psychics; but later on the *choïkoi* rejoiced under that appellation, when *pistis* had become degraded to mean "faith" in the sense of blind credulity.

[2] Gr. *eikôn*, an image, figure, statue; resemblance; phantom, spectre, wraith.

[3] The physical body of the unpurified man is patterned after the lunar form, that of the Initiate after the solar form. As the lunar body usually perishes after the death of the physical, the choïk man changes in appearance from incarnation to incarnation, whereas the Initiate preserves much the same semblance whenever incarnated.

tible. Behold, I tell you a Mystery[1]: we shall not all sleep, but we shall all be transformed, in the Atom,[2] in an out-flashing of an Eye,[3] in the last trumpet-call.[4] For a trumpet shall sound, and the dead ones shall be raised indestructible, and *we* shall be transformed. For this

[1] Gr. *mustêrion*, an arcane teaching, a secret. By the word "Behold" Paulos directs attention to the inner meaning of his words. In the Greater Mysteries (*ta megala*) the Initiate became a Seer or beholder (*epoptês*) of the realities of Nature and Super-Nature; but in the Lesser Mysteries (*ta mikra*) the teaching was imparted orally and by means of dramatic representations, allegorically setting forth the descent of the Soul from the world of real Being into the transition-sphere and world of matter, its remedial discipline and purification, and its final return to the divine state. These representations degenerated into public entertainments, with Tragedies and Comedies. In the Christian system dramas were instituted, in which the life and crucifixion of Iêsous were enacted; and from these the modern theatre had its origin.

[2] In allusion to the atomic (non-molecular) nature of the pneumatic body. The rendering "moment," "atom [of time]," has no warrant in the Greek language.

[3] Referring to the "third eye," the seventh brain-centre, from which the pneumatic body is projected. See note 1, p. 200.

[4] The last of the seven trumpet-calls, or mystic sounds heard as the Breath impinges successively upon the seven brain-centres. In the *Apokalypse* the "woman veiled with the Sun" appears after the seventh Messenger has sounded his trumpet, and she gives birth to the man-child, the Christos.

destroyed must be clothed with indestructibility, and this mortal must be clothed with immortality. Now, when this destroyed shall have been clothed with indestructibility, and this mortal shall have been clothed with immortality, then shall come to pass that saying which is written: "Death is swallowed up in victory. Where, O Death,[1] is your goad? Where, O Under-world,[2] is your victory?"[3] The goad of Death is sin, and the force of sin is the Law.[4]

[1] The physical world, or world of death.

[2] Gr. *hadês*, the nether-world, the realm into which the soul passes after the death of the physical body, and where it is purged of its grosser impurities before ascending to the spiritual world. But when the soul returns to reincarnate, it passes again through this sphere and has to resume the impure elements from which it was temporarily freed. Also during the sleep of the physical body the soul goes into Hadês, as well as at death. When the soul has become freed from the cycle of reincarnations through the "birth from above," it is said to "have the keys of Hadês and of Death." Hadês is not a place of punishment, but of purification, and in its higher planes it corresponds to, or rather merges into, Paradise (*paradeisos*, pleasure-garden).

[3] *Isa.* xxv. 8; *Hos.* xiii. 14.

[4] The soul is kept in the bondage of birth by its mistaking the seeming for the real, and this glamour is the force (*dunamis*) of the Law. See note 3, p. 78.

INDEX OF NOTES.

Abiding, 3, 174.
Above, 2, 94.
Accuser, 1, 125.
Adversary, 2, 173.
Advocate, 1, 176.
Air, 2, 82.
Amên, 3, 88.
Anointed, 1, 79.
Awakening, 2, 112; 1, 157.

Believe, 3, 74.
Blood, 2, 82.
Breath, 2, 84.

Circumcision, 4, 128.
Class, 2, 160.
Cleansing, 1, 99.
Come into being, 1, 73; 1, 180.
Commonplace, 1, 150.

Darkness, 1, 74.
Dead, 1, 93; 2, 94.
Death, 1, 112.
Dust, 1, 225.

Earth, 1, 96.
Ecstatic, 1, 114.

Faith, 3, 74.
Fire, 2, 82; 3, 82.
First, 2, 78; 1, 84.
First-principle, 1, 71.
Fulness, 2, 78.

Ghost, 2, 151.
God, 1, 72; 2, 72.
Grace, 4, 77.

Hêlias, 3, 80.
Hermês, 1, 151.
Hierousalém, 1, 80.

Immortal, 2, 171.
Ixion, 2, 137.

Judge, 1, 97.

Law, 3, 78.
Leader, 1, 94.
Life, 2, 73.
Light, 1, 74.
Love, 3, 111; 3, 114; 1, 212.
Lustrate, 2, 82.

Man, 3, 73.
Messages, 2, 104.
Messenger, 4, 88.
Messias, 1, 75; 3, 115.
Mystery, 1, 226.

Name, 4, 76; 3, 88.

On-going, 4, 96.

Passing-over, 2, 91; 3, 194.
Path, 2, 81; 1, 175.
Perfect, 2, 105.
Perfecting-period, 1, 170.
Petros, 1, 86.
Portents, 2, 107.

Radiance, 2, 77; 1, 115.
Realm, 3, 94.
Recorders, 4, 132.
Ruler, 2, 88.

229

Sabbath, 1, 110.
Save, 2, 97; 3, 115; 1, 156.
Saviour, 3, 106.
Saying, 3, 93.
Season, 1, 109.
Seer, 1, 81; 1, 161.
Self-born, 3, 77.
Separate, 1, 97.
Sign, 1, 91.
Sin, 2, 83.
Sky, 3, 84; 1, 221.
Spook, 1, 128; 1, 142.
Substance, 1, 219.

Tent-making, 3, 125.
Thought, 2, 71.

True, 1, 75; 5, 100.
Truth, 1, 78.

Under-world, 2, 227.
Useless, 1, 2, 98.

Voice, 1, 95.

Water, 2, 82; 3, 82.
Wheel of Birth, 2, 137.
Witness, 2, 74.
Words, 6, 100.
Works, 3, 97.
World, 2, 75.
Wrath, 1, 101.
Writing, 2, 93.

ABOUT THE AUTHOR

James Morgan Pryse (1859 – 1942) was an author, publisher, and theosophist. Pryse was born in New London, Ohio (a suburb of Cincinnati), and died in Los Angeles, California.

James began his career in law, but gave it up for journalism. In adult life he travelled extensively, helping create a utopian colony in Topolobampo, Mexico, and editing the Topolobampo periodical from his New Jersey home.

James settled in Los Angeles, California in 1886. He joined the Los Angeles branch of the Theosophical Society on July 28, 1887. His brother John was already a member at that time. John later dropped out of the Theosophical Society and founded the Gnostic Society in 1928. The original headquarters of the Gnostic Society was in John's home in Los Angeles.

In July 1888 the Pryse brothers arrived in New York City. In 1889, members of the Theosophical Society from New York City and Chicago purchased a printing press and type, for the purpose of setting up a publishing company which would handle the publishing needs of the various branches of the Theosophical Society located in the United States. This theosophical publishing company, named the Aryan Press, was located at 144 Madison Avenue in Manhattan, New York City. James was recruited to set up and operate the Aryan Press, which was in full operation by December 1889.

Due to the success of the Aryan Press, a larger printing press was purchased and shipped to London, England. In August 1890, James was contacted by Helena Blavatsky (co-founder of the Theosophical Society) and summoned to London, for the purpose of setting up and operating this new publishing company, known as the H. P. B. Press (Printers to the Theosophical Society). This printing press was also referred to as the "Blavatsky Press." James left New York City for London in September 1890, at which time his brother John took over operation of the Aryan Press. The H. P. B. Press (Blavatsky Press) was installed in London about November 1890.

Blavatsky had asked James to publish her *Esoteric Instructions* in the United States, so the work would be accessible to members of the American branches of the Theosophical Society. Blavatsky's *Esoteric Instructions* was duly published by the Aryan Press in 1890.

In *The Apocalypse Unsealed* (1910) Pryse published the secret key to decoding the esoteric meaning of the Biblical *Book of Revelation*. His *The Restored New Testament* (1914) also shows esoteric meaning.

Publications of James Morgan Pryse:

- *"Credit Foncier of Sinaloa: As a Solution of the Labor Question"*, Credit Foncier of Sinaloa, Vol. 2, Issue 20 (1886), 8 pages.
- *The Sermon on the Mount and Other Extracts from the New Testament: A Verbatim Translation from the Greek, with Notes on the Mystical or Arcane Sense* (New York: Elliott B. Page & Co., 1899)
- *Reincarnation in the New Testament* (1900)
- *The Magical Message according to Iôannês (To kata Iôannĕn Euangelion): Commonly called the Gospel according to (St.) John - A Verbatim Translation from the Greek done in Modern English, with Introductory Essays and Notes* (New York: Theosophical Publishing Co. of New York, 1909)
- *The Apocalypse Unsealed, being an Esoteric Interpretation of the Initiation of Iôannês* (New

York: J. M. Pryse, 1910)

- *The Restored New Testament, the Hellenic Fragments, freed from the pseudo-Jewish Interpolations, Harmonized, and done into English Verse and Prose with Introductory Analyses, and Commentaries, giving Interpretation according to Ancient Philosophy and Psychology and New Literal Translation of the Synoptic Gospels, with Introduction and Commentaries* (New York: J. M. Pryse; London: J. M. Watkins, 1914)

- *The Adorers of Dionysos (Bakchai), translated from the Greek of Euripides; with an Original Interpretation of the Myth of Kadmos* (Los Angeles: John M. Pryse; London: John M. Watkins, 1925)

- *A New Presentation of the Prometheus Bound of Aischylos, wherein is set forth the Hidden Meaning of the Myth* (Los Angeles: J. M. Pryse; London: John M. Watkins, 1925).

- *Spiritual Light: New Scripture by Many Authors and Translations from Ancient Manuscripts, Previously Unpublished* (Los Angeles: John M. Pryse, 1940, 192 pages)